# 303
# TRICKY
# CHECKMATES

## 2, 3 & 4 MOVE CHECKMATES!

# 303 TRICKY CHECKMATES

## 2, 3 & 4 MOVE CHECKMATES!

**FRED WILSON & BRUCE ALBERSTON**

CARDOZA PUBLISHING

## ACKNOWLEDGMENTS

Special thanks to our secret resource, Michele Lance. Michele stopped short of chopping wood to make paper, but she was involved in everything else. Others who contributed positions, checked solutions, or made useful suggestions include: Christopher Mayfield, David MacEnulty, Adam Marcus, Gregory Caesar, Dan Satterwaite, Ben Schanback, Jeff Tannenbaum, Tom Schrade, Mike Senkiewicz, Emmitt Jefferson, Andy Ansel, Andrew Fox, Glen Hart, Ned Wall, Oshon Temple, Rita Kelly, Marianna Loosemore and Larry Grasso.

---

**2018 NEW EDITION**

Library of Congress Catalog Card No: 2017964675
ISBN: 978-1-58042-364-9

Visit our web site—www.cardozabooks.com—or write for a full list of books and computer strategies.

---

### CARDOZA PUBLISHING
P.O. Box 98115, Las Vegas, NV 89193
Phone (800) 577-WINS
email: cardozabooks@aol.com

# ABOUT THE AUTHORS

## FRED WILSON
Fred Wilson is among the finest chess teachers and authors. Wilson has authored *303 Tricky Chess Tactics*, *303 Tricky Chess Puzzles*, *303 Crushing Chess Tactics*, and *303 Tricky Checkmates* with Bruce Alberston for Cardoza Publishing. He is the owner of Fred Wilson Chess Books in New York City.

## BRUCE ALBERSTON
Bruce Alberston, a well-known chess trainer and teacher in the New York City area, collaborated with Fred Wilson on *202 Surprising Mates*, *303 Tricky Chess Tactics*, *303 Tricky Chess Puzzles*, *303 Crushing Chess Tactics*, and *303 Tricky Checkmates* with Wilson. He is also the sole author of two books: *51 Chess Openings* and *Savage Chess Opening Traps*. Alberston did significant research and analysis for Bruce Pandolfini (who has written 17 books for Simon & Shuster).

# TABLE OF CONTENTS

# SYMBOLS AND ABBREVIATIONS

**K** stands for King
**Q** stands for Queen
**R** stands for Rook
**B** stands for Bishop
**N** stands for Knight
**There** is no symbol for the pawn. A pawn move is indicated by a lowercase letter which identifies the file of the moving pawn. (e4 shows that a pawn has moved to the e4 square. If a capital letter had preceded the letter, such as Ne4, it would shows a piece had moved there, in this case, the Knight.)

---

**x** stands for a capture
**0-0** stands for King-side castling
**0-0-0** stands for Queen-side castling

---

**...** the three dots following a move number indicate a Black move. (2...e6 indicates that Black's second move was to bring the pawn to e6.)
**/** with a capital letter immediately to the right of the slash mark indicates that a pawn is promoted to a piece. (h1/Q shows that the pawn on the h file moved to the h1 square – thus a Black pawn – and was promoted to a Queen.)

---

**+** stands for check
**#** stands for checkmate

---

**!** means very good move
**!!** means brilliant move
**?** means bad move
**??** means losing blunder

# INTRODUCTION

"I can't believe I missed a mate in two!" How many, many times have you said this to yourself during your chessplaying career? Too often, I bet. Deep down you know that missed tactical threats or opportunities are the biggest hindrance to your improvement at chess.

Recently, one of us, Fred Wilson, reached the following position as White:

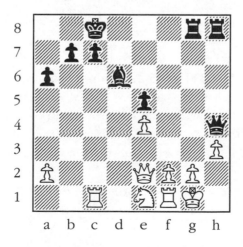

**11**

White, although a Pawn ahead, has a difficult position because of Black's heavy artillery on the g and h files, pointing at his King. Among Black's threats, were it his move, are 1... Qxh3 with a winning attack. White's g Pawn is pinned against his King by the Black Rook on g8.

White had a choice between 1. Qf3, which, although it defends against possible sacrifices on g2, does lose the h Pawn to 1... Qxh3! 2. Qxh3 Rxh3, and the seemingly safe, 1. Kh1, which is what he did.

What would you do now if you were Black?

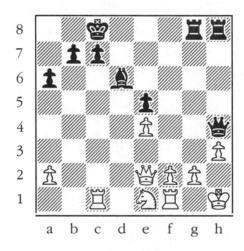

Answer: **1... Qxh3+! gxh3 2. Rxh3#.** That's right! An experienced player fell into a classic *corridor mate*, wherein the doomed King is mated by a major piece (Queen or Rook) on a rank or file, because there are no legal escape squares on the adjacent ranks or files, and no possible interpositions.

The possibility of this classic mating pattern, (like the notorious *back rank mate* except here mate occurs on the h file rather then the 1st or 8th rank,) should have been recognized by White, even if it was brought about by a Queen sacrifice!

So, what's the answer? How can we learn to stop overlooking mating combinations available to us, and threatened against us? There is only one way: to study different types of checkmating combinations over and over again until we are thoroughly familiar with the tactics and typical groups of pieces involved in successfully implementing them.

While in the past, it was believed that the ability to create attractive checkmating combinations must be a born gift, nowadays modern teaching experience has established that consistent training through solving standard checkmating positions, no matter how difficult, will improve any player's "feel" for discovering correct, and even brilliant, checkmating attacks.

What we have done in *303 Tricky Checkmates* is to assemble a collection of *forced* checkmates in 2, 3 and 4 moves, which we believe you will find both instructive and entertaining. We have purposely used very large, clear diagrams so you will not be discouraged from really trying to visualize possible variations.

We have also intentionally included 100 positions (mates 101-150 and 251-300), in which Black is to play and force checkmate in two or three moves. We believe it is essential that you become comfortable with looking at positions from Black's perspective and solving tough tactical problems from that side.

Our classifcation system is quite direct in that we most often tell you, under the "theme column" in the introductions to Chapters One and Three, exactly what pieces and/or Pawns are creating the mate. For instance, Position No. 17 in Chapter One is a classic Rook plus Bishop corridor mate on the 8th rank and we urge you to look at it right now and solve it!

Hint: the solution begins with a **quiet move,** a move that is neither a check nor a capture, which is why quiet moves are often the hardest to find.

**Queen support mate** simply means that you are mating the enemy King by placing your Queen next to it, with another one of your pieces or Pawns also attacking the mating square which you have just placed your Queen on. An example of this is the following position where, with White to move, the Spanish master Vilardebo missed an opportunity to checkmate one of the world's greatest players, Richard Reti, at the First Chess Olympiad, London 1927.

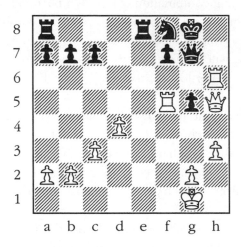

What would you have played? Notice that Black's Queen is what we call **overloaded** in that it has to defend against mates on both h8 and f7. We hope you found the answer: **1. Rh8+!** (a classic *deflection*, making the Queen give up her defense of f7). **1...Qxh8 forced, 2. Qxf7#.**

A **discovery** is any move by a piece or Pawn which opens a line of fire onto the enemy King, via a rank, file or diagonal, from a piece lurking behind the just moved unit. The most devastating discoveries are usually **double checks**, as in the example below where White mates in three moves.

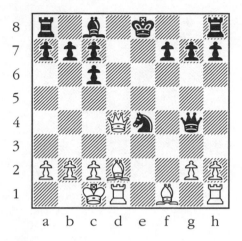

This looks really tough, but during an offhand game in Paris, 1878, Maczulsky created a spectacular checkmate against Kolisch by means of a deadly discovered double check: **1. Qd8+!! Kxd8; 2. Bg5+ Ke8; 3. Rd8#.**

Although you may already know what a *pin* is in chess, you may not be sure how pins can be used tactically to force checkmate. We suggest you go immediately to Positions 79 and 80 in Chapter One. In each of these examples, White forces mate in two moves by creating a murderous pin by sacrificing a piece.

Now, we come to what is probably the most difficult tactical concept of all, especially when it is used to force checkmate, namely the "dreaded" zugswang. **Zugswang** basically means "compulsion to move". The losing side must make a move, but would rather not because the only legal moves available cause immediate loss.

Consider the following:

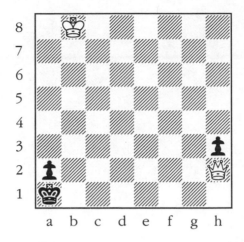

It is White's move. Would you grab the h Pawn or...? We certainly hope not because then the position is theoretically a draw! But, perhaps you noticed that after 1. Qc2!, Black is not only not *stalemated* as he would have been had there been no h Pawn, but is, in fact, in *zugswang*, as his only legal move 1... h2, allows 2. Qc1#.

Finally, you will notice that throughout the book there are an abundance of sacrifices. Particularly evident and exciting are the Queen sacrifices to open lines of attack, to annihilate defenders, to draw off or deflect defenders, or to attract the King to the mating square.

The whole tactical canon of chess is condensed in the challenging mates you will find in this book.

Enjoy.

Fred Wilson & Bruce Alberston

# CHAPTER 1

## WHITE TO MOVE AND MATE IN TWO

## WHITE MATES IN TWO

"White mates in two" indicates that White moves first, Black responds, and White delivers checkmate on his second move. Computer people think of this as three individual moves, or three-ply. Chess folks, accustomed to thinking in move pairs, refer to this as a two-mover. Technically, it's just a move and a half, as Black never gets to make his second move.

## ORGANIZATION

The layout of Chapter One is by theme. Typical mating configurations and strategems are grouped together to aid familiarization. Here's what to look for:

| Problems | Theme |
|----------|-------|
| 1-13 | Back rank and other corridor mates |
| 14-27 | Rook and Bishop corridors |
| 28-39 | Diagonal mates with Queen and Bishop or Rook and Bishop or only a Bishop! |
| 40-48 | Bishop and Knight Mates |
| 49-64 | Support mates with the Queen |
| 65-73 | Knight checkmates |
| 74-78 | Pawn mates and promotion |
| 79-92 | Pins and discoveries |
| 93-100 | Quiet moves and Zugswang |

## SOLVING HINTS

Since the goal is checkmate and you have only two moves to work with, you'll need to operate with forcing moves. The most forcing moves are also the most violent moves: checks, captures and immediate threats of mate. Also, don't be afraid to sacrifice. Material becomes irrelevant when you're hunting down the enemy King.

Go to it now and get the enemy King.

**1.**

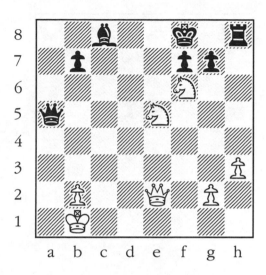

**2.**

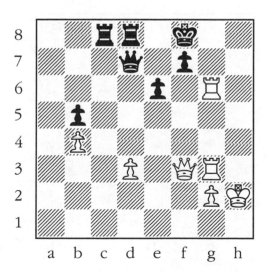

**3.**

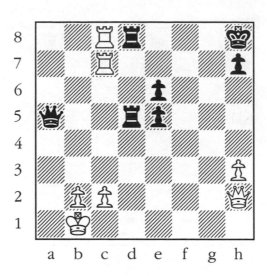

**4.**

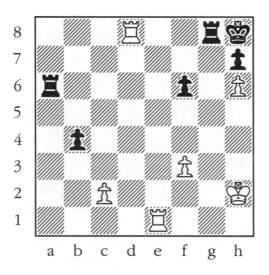

**5.**

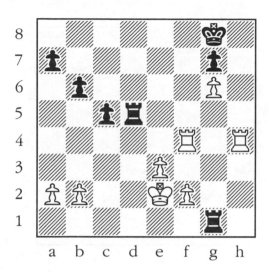

**6.**

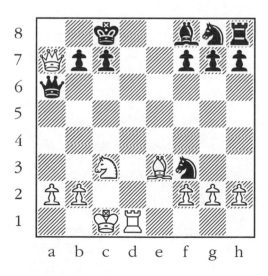

**7.**

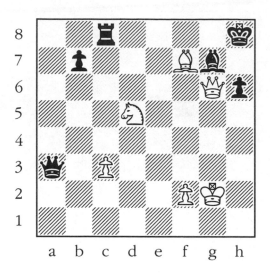

**8.**

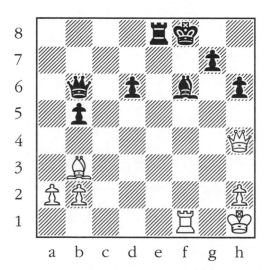

**9.**

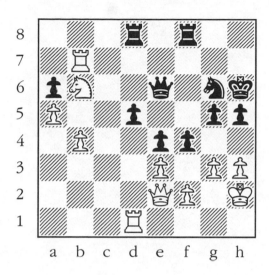

**10.**

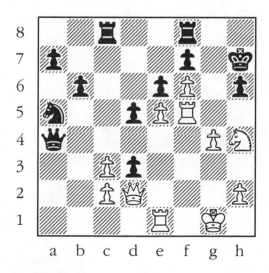

## 11.

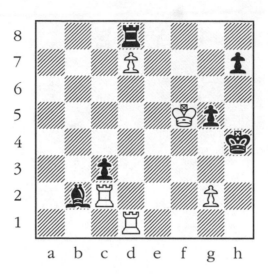

## 12.

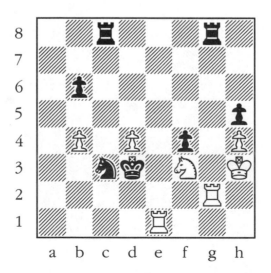

## 13.

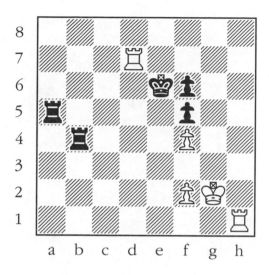

## 14.

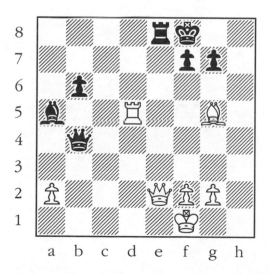

## 15.

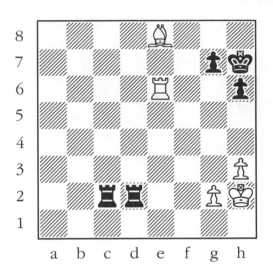

## 16.

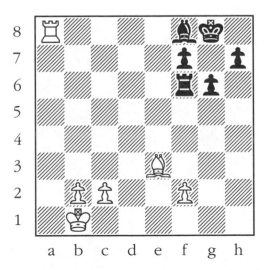

**17.**

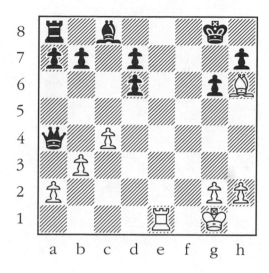

**18.**

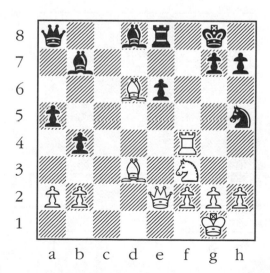

**19.**

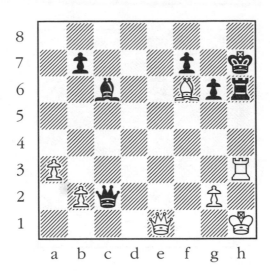

**20.**

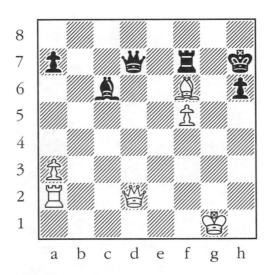

**21.**

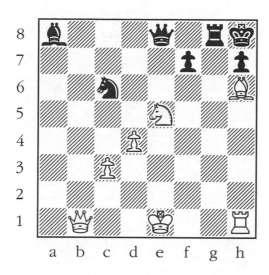

**22.**

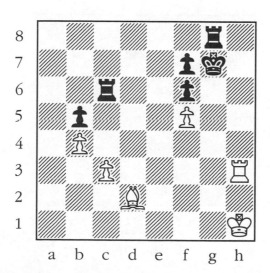

## 23.

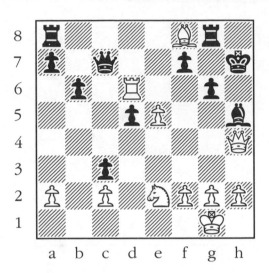

## 24.

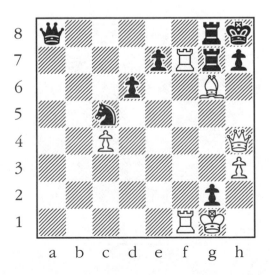

**25.**

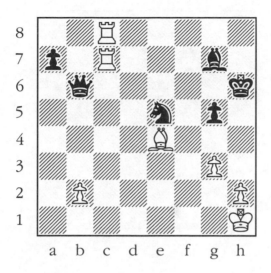

**26.**

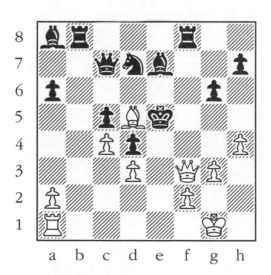

## 27.

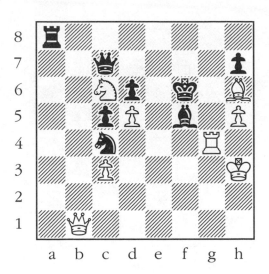

## 28.

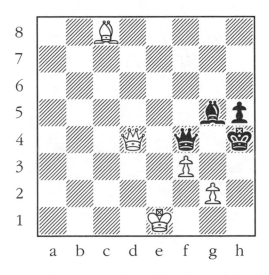

## 29.

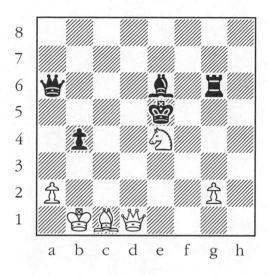

## 30.

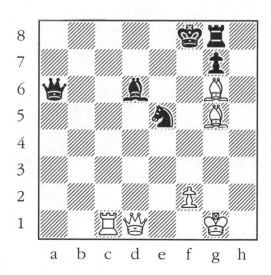

## 31.

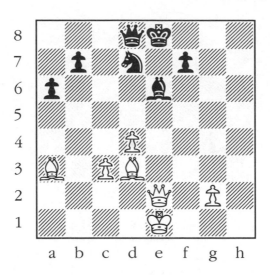

## 32.

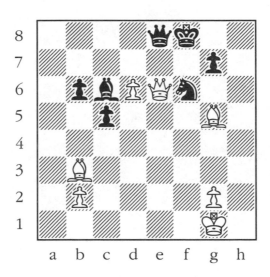

**33.**

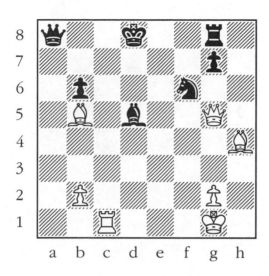

**34.**

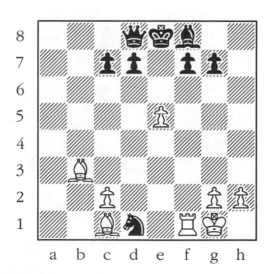

**35.**

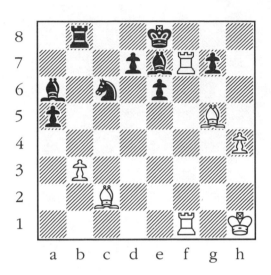

**36.**

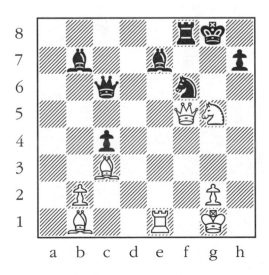

**37.**

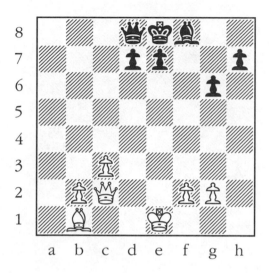

**38.**

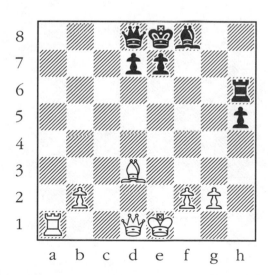

**39.**

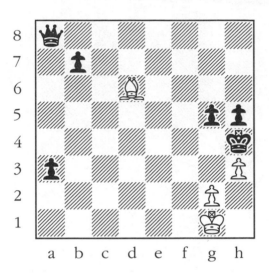

**40.**

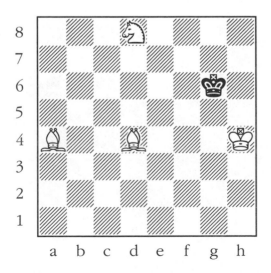

## 41.

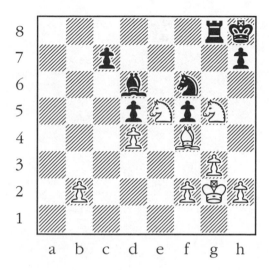

## 42.

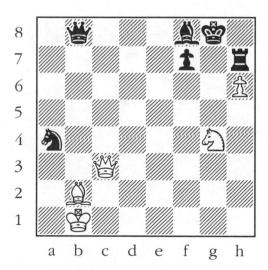

**43.**

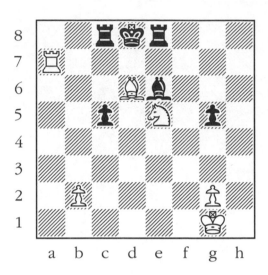

**44.**

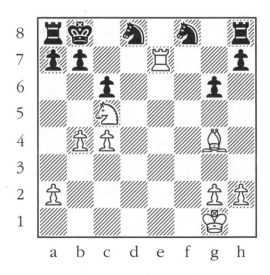

## 45.

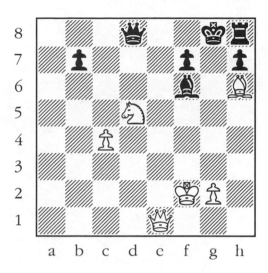

## 46.

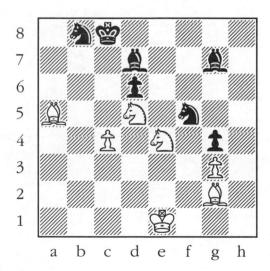

## 47.

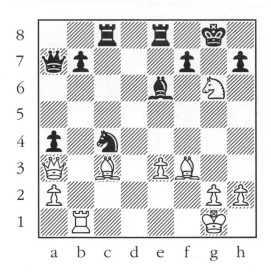

## 48.

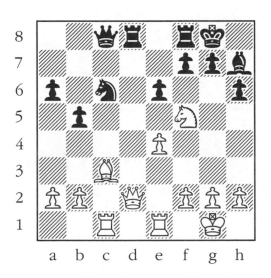

**49.**

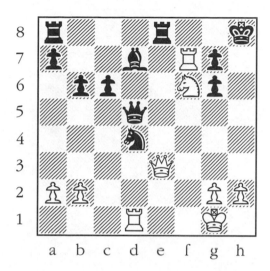

**50.**

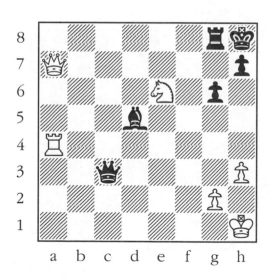

## 51.

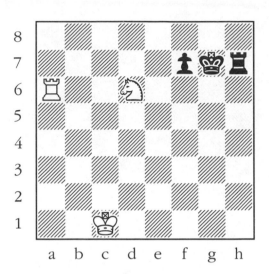

## 52.

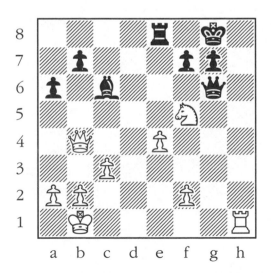

## 53.

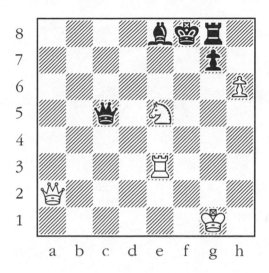

## 54.

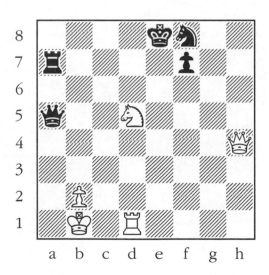

## 55.

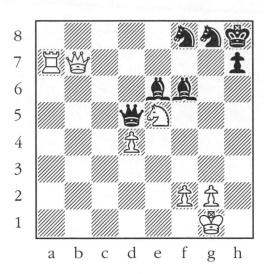

## 56.

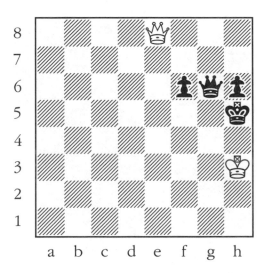

**57.**

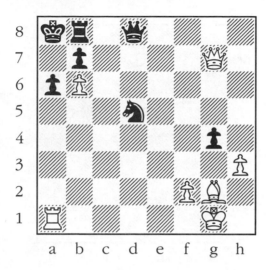

**58.**

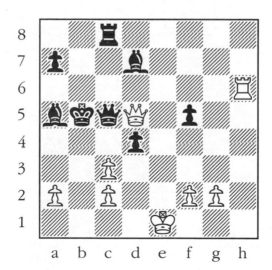

**59.**

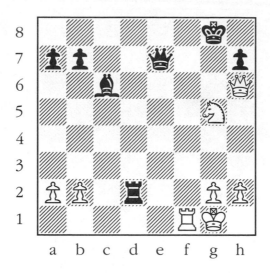

**60.**

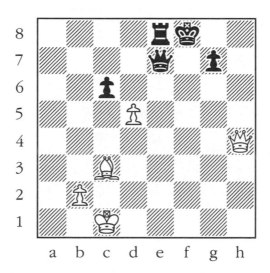

**61.**

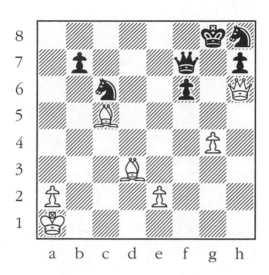

**62.**

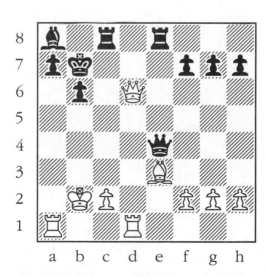

**63.**

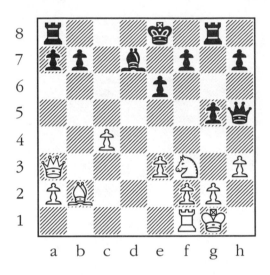

**64.**

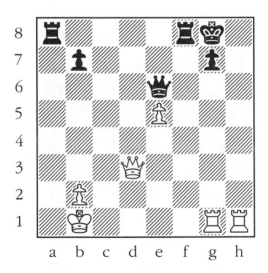

**65.**

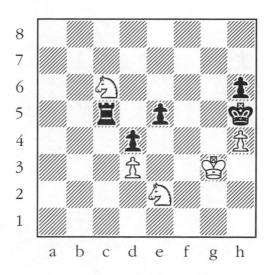

**66.**

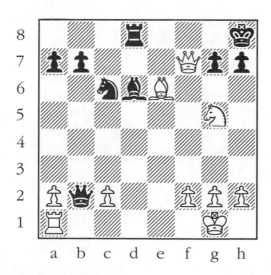

**67.**

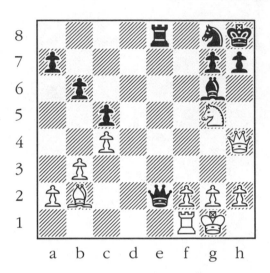

**68.**

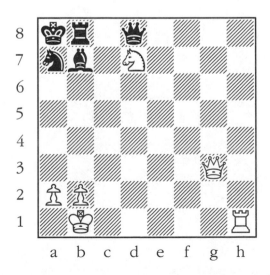

**69.**

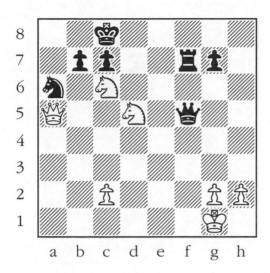

**70.**

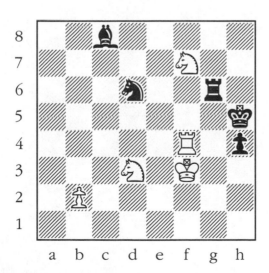

**71.**

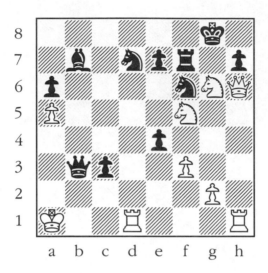

**72.**

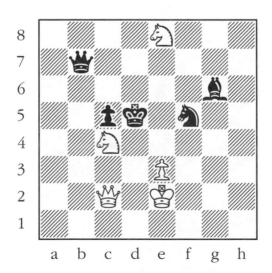

**73.**

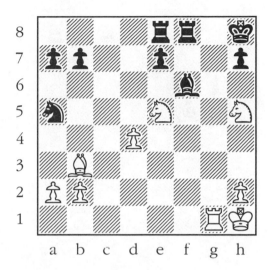

**74.**

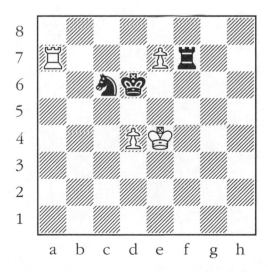

**75.**

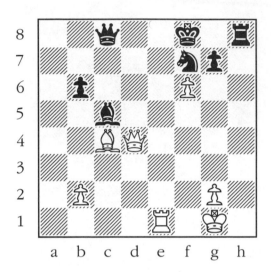

**76.**

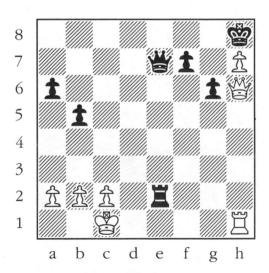

**77.**

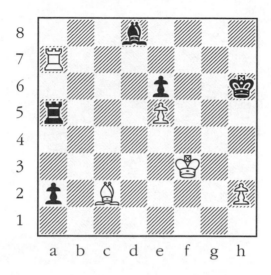

**78.**

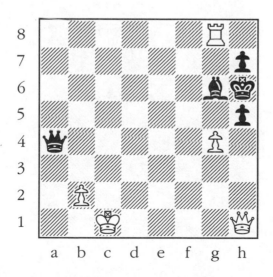

## 79.

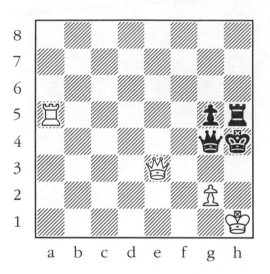

## 80.

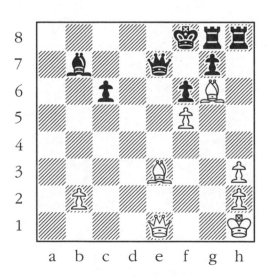

### 81.

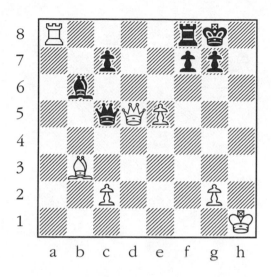

### 82.

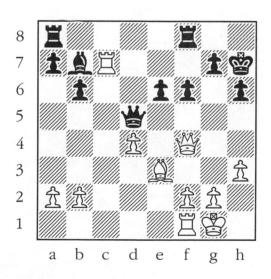

**83.**

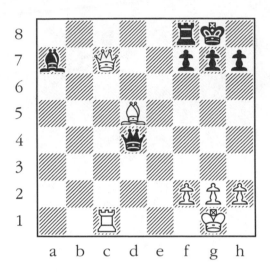

**84.**

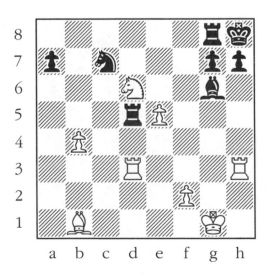

## 85.

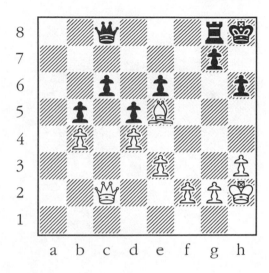

## 86.

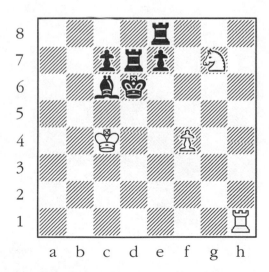

## 87.

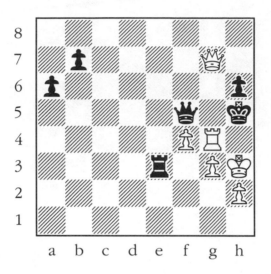

## 88.

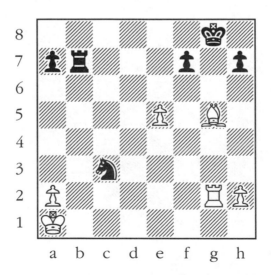

**89.**

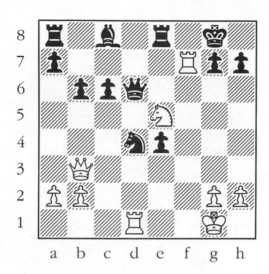

**90.**

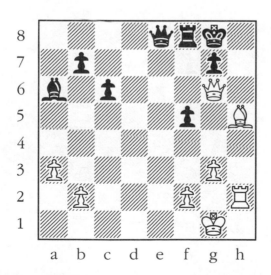

## 91.

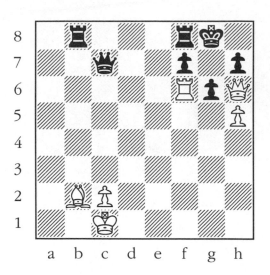

## 92.

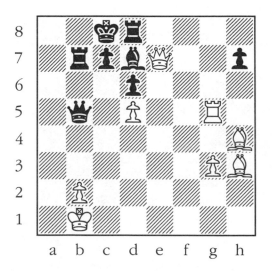

**93.**

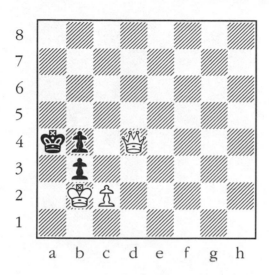

**94.**

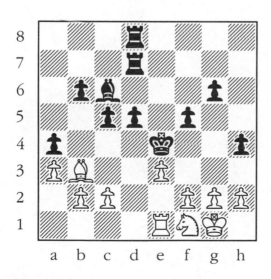

**95.**

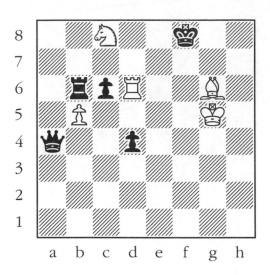

**96.**

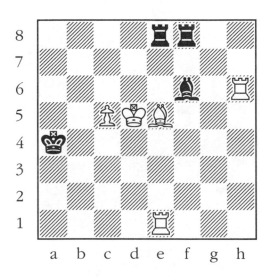

**97.**

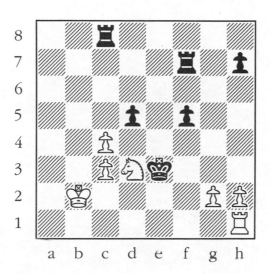

**98.**

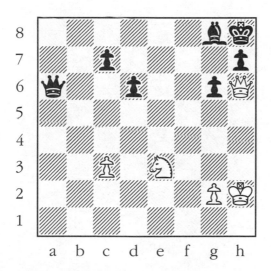

**99.**

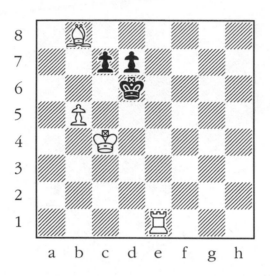

**100.**

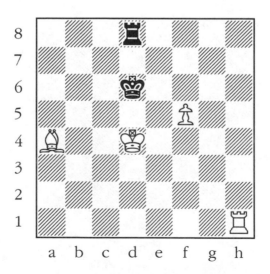

# CHAPTER 2

## BLACK TO MOVE AND MATE IN TWO

### BLACK MATES IN TWO

Here Black gets to make the first move, or the *key move* as it is sometimes called. White replies, and Black administers checkmate on his second move. There's nothing unusual about viewing the position from Black's perspective. In chess games, you'll have the Black pieces half the time. And Black also wins his share of the games.

### ORGANIZATION

The mates are organized randomly, deliberately so. You're expected to see your way without any prompting. But here at least, as opposed to an actual game situation, you have the advantage of knowing mate is imminent.

In general, the problems in this section are harder than those in the previous one. More imagination is required and there are more side variations to consider. By this stage, however, most of the patterns should already be familiar, so it's a matter of applying what you already know.

### SOLVING HINTS

As in the last chapter, forcing moves are the order of the day. Checks and captures with checks abound. Material sacrifice is by now a commonplace occurrence. The idea is to make the position bend to your will. Forcing moves will do it.

Problem #132 comes from our dirty tricks department. You'll need to know two things: the *en passant* capture, and White's last move, b2-b4.

Positions #130 and #140 are composed problems. They are included here more for their curiosity than for anything else. In each, Black places a piece on a square where it can be captured in multiple ways. Each mode of capture weakens the White defense in some fashion, allowing Black to mate. A methodical approach to these mates work best.

You are ready to begin Chapter Two. The objective is the White monarch. Go after him.

## 101.

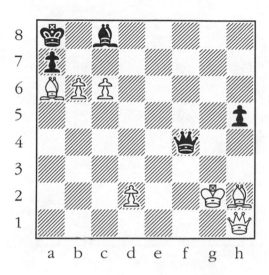

## 102.

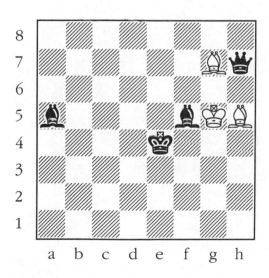

**103.**

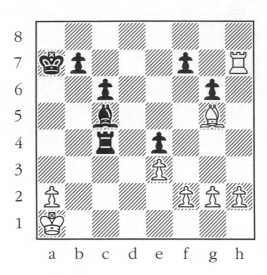

**104.**

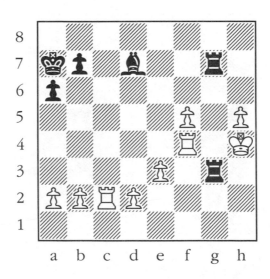

### 105.

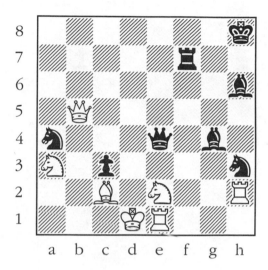

### 106.

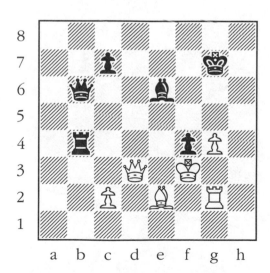

## 107.

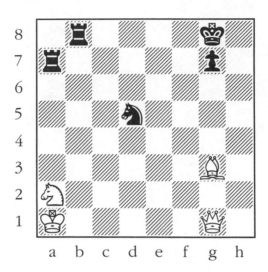

## 108.

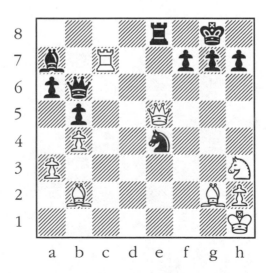

## 109.

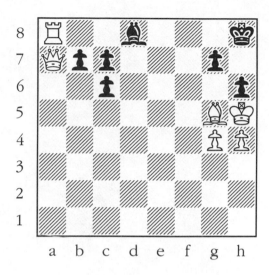

## 110.

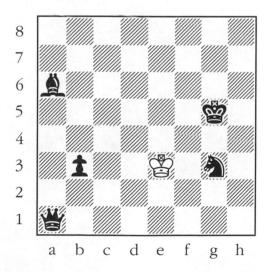

## 111.

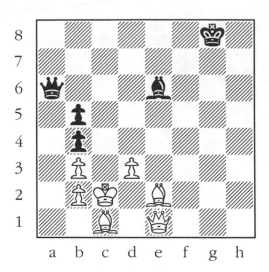

## 112.

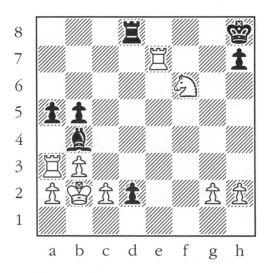

### 113.

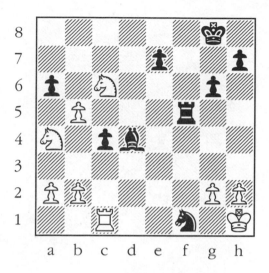

### 114.

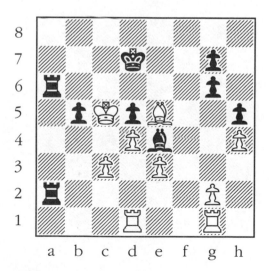

## 115.

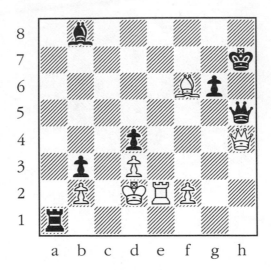

## 116.

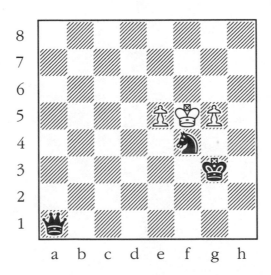

**117.**

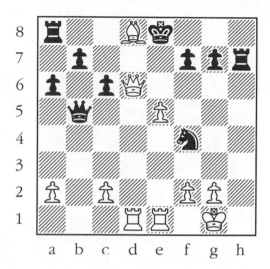

**118.**

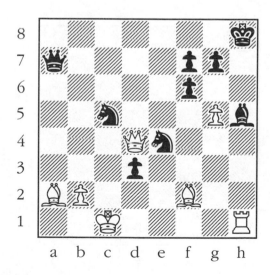

## 119.

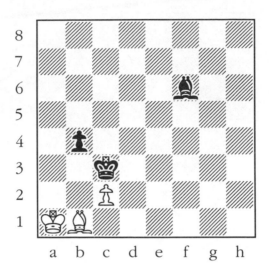

## 120.

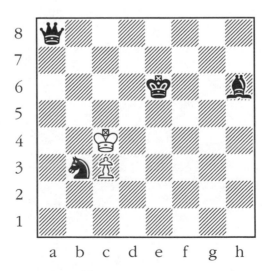

**121.**

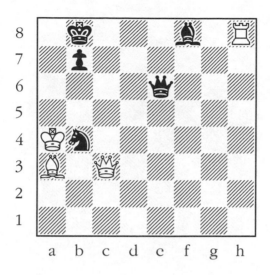

**122.**

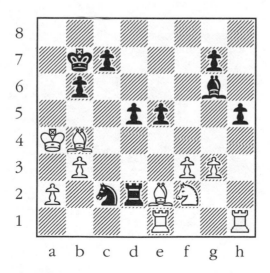

## 123.

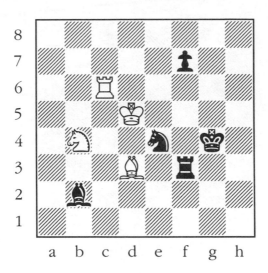

## 124.

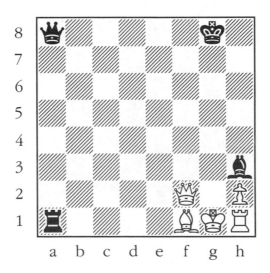

## 125.

## 126.

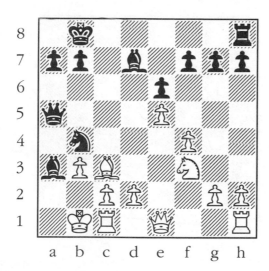

## 127.

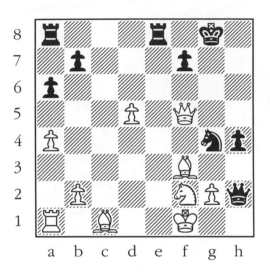

## 128.

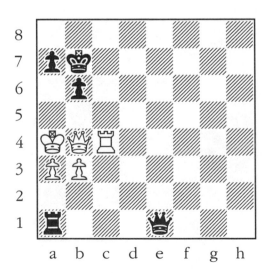

## 129.

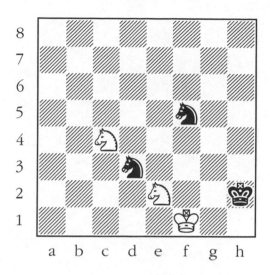

## 130.

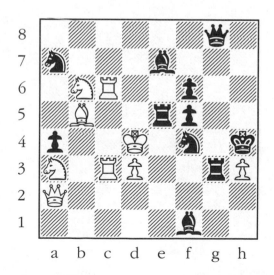

## 131.

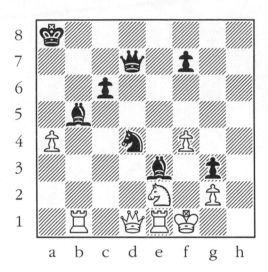

## 132.

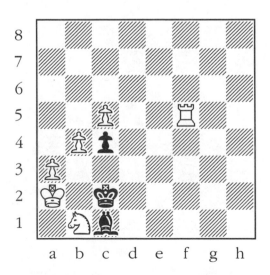

**133.**

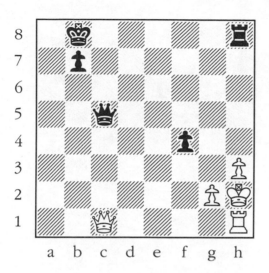

**134.**

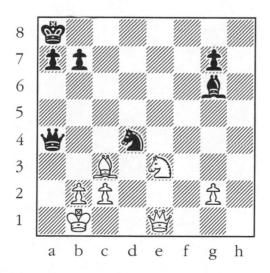

## 135.

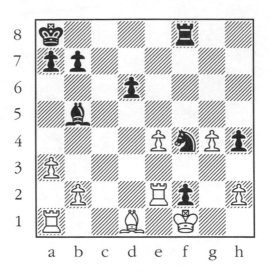

## 136.

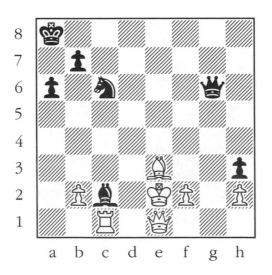

## 137.

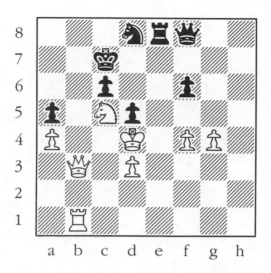

## 138.

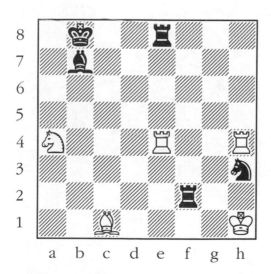

**139.**

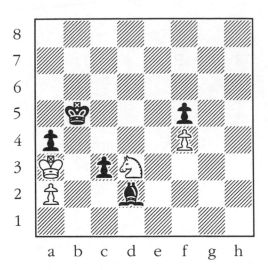

**140.**

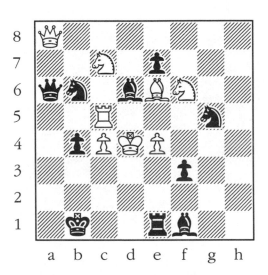

**141.**

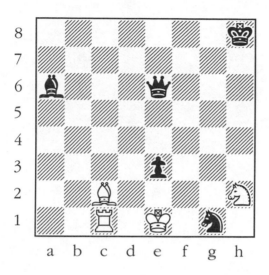

**142.**

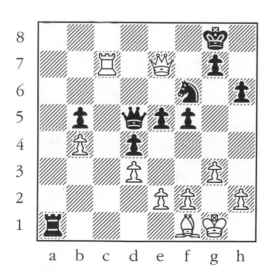

## 143.

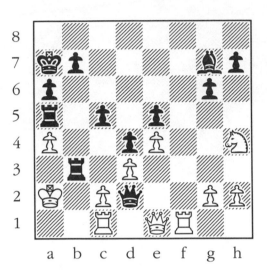

## 144.

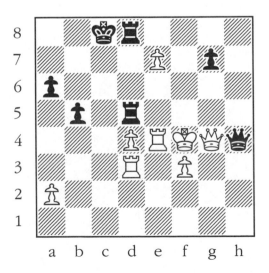

## 145.

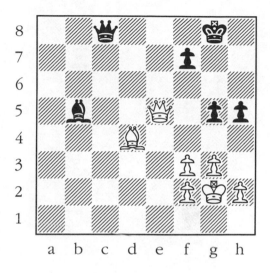

## 146.

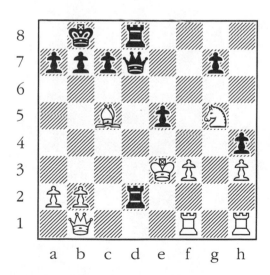

## 147.

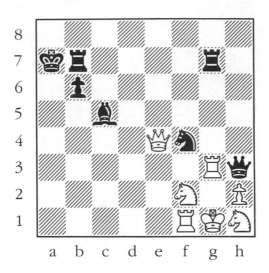

## 148.

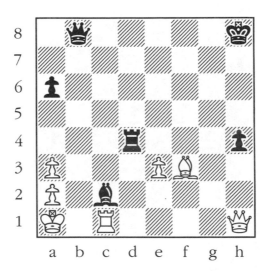

**149.**

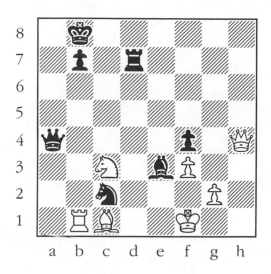

**150.**

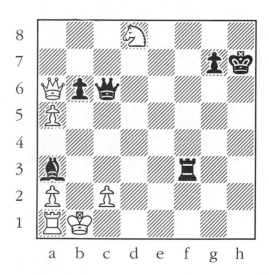

# CHAPTER 3

## WHITE TO MOVE AND MATE IN THREE

### WHITE MATES IN THREE

In this chapter, it is White's turn to initiate the action: White moves, Black moves, White moves, Black moves, White's third move is checkmate. White uses moves one and two to open lines for his pieces, eliminate defenders, take away escape squares from the enemy King – in short, everything necessary to insure that move three is mate.

### ORGANIZATION

The fundamental ideas of chess are fairly constant, thus, the catagories in this chapter look pretty much like those in Chapter One. But the numerous ways of implementing those basic ideas is where these mates get interesting.

| Problems | Theme |
|----------|-------|
| 151-170 | Back rank and other corridors |
| 171-177 | Rook and Bishop corridors |
| 178-185 | Bishop combinations: Q&B; N&B; 2 Bs. |
| 186-193 | Rook and Knight Mates |
| 194-212 | Queen support mates |
| 213-220 | Knight mates |
| 221-228 | Promotion and pawn mates |
| 229-243 | Pins and discoveries |
| 244-250 | Quiet moves and Zugswang |

## SOLVING HINTS

We've advanced from the two mover to the three mover. In many instances, this is merely a lengthening of the mating process, a one move extension of a two move idea. Number 160 is a case in point. At its core, #160 is essentially the same as the two-mover, #15. But just as often, there is an extra dimension, a concept that cannot be carried out in less than three moves.

Your task then: extend and conceptualize to mate.

**151.**

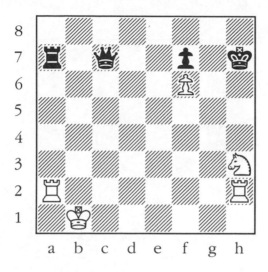

**152.**

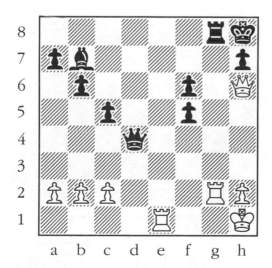

**153.**

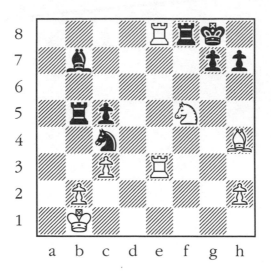

**154.**

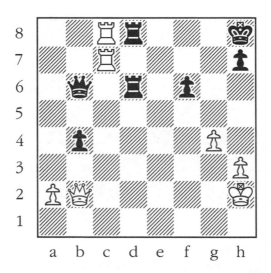

**155.**

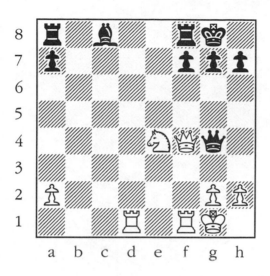

**156.**

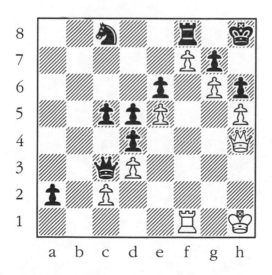

**157.**

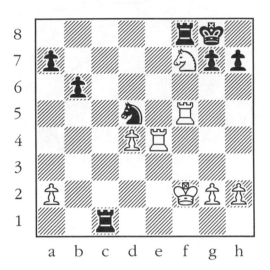

**158.**

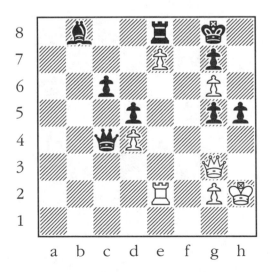

## 159.

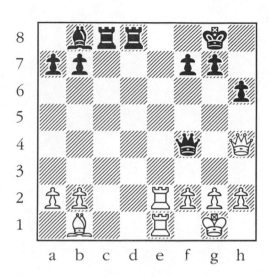

## 160.

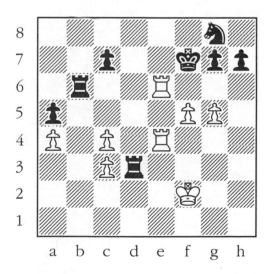

## 161.

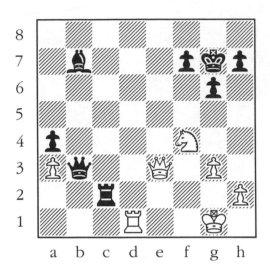

## 162.

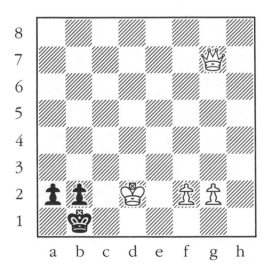

### 163.

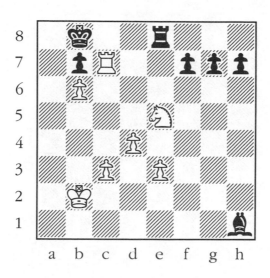

### 164.

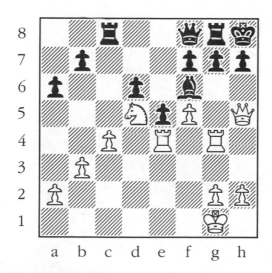

**165.**

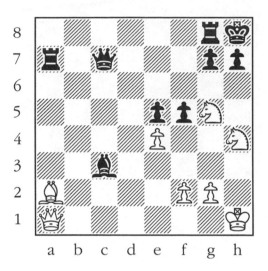

**166.**

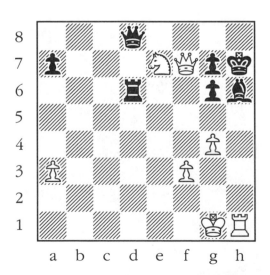

**167.**

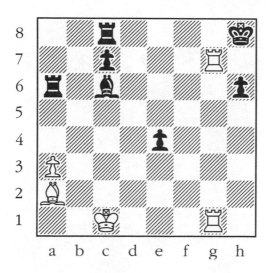

**168.**

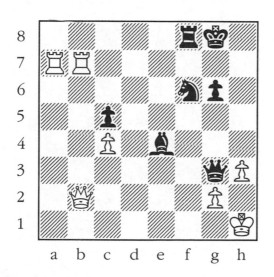

**169.**

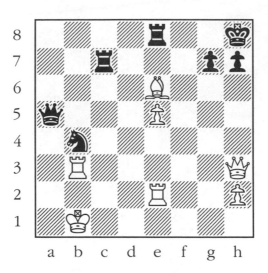

**170.**

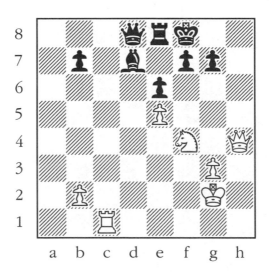

**171.**

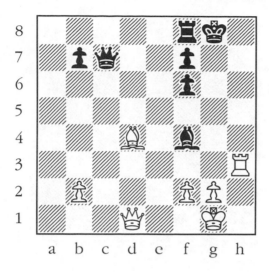

**172.**

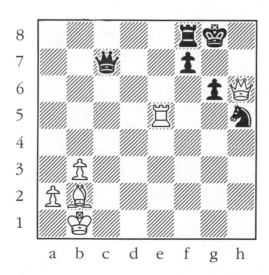

## 173.

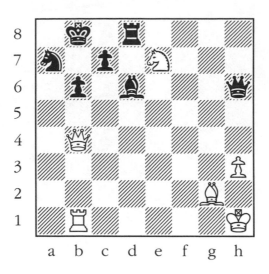

## 174.

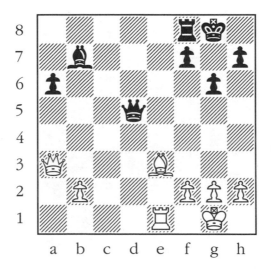

**175.**

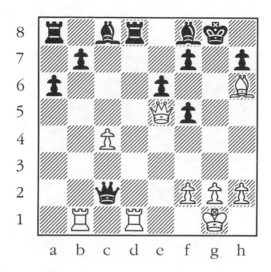

**176.**

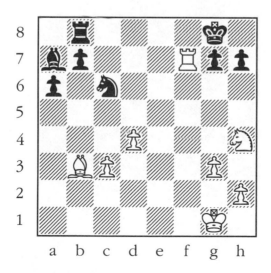

**177.**

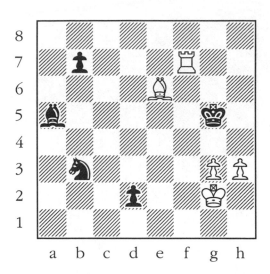

**178.**

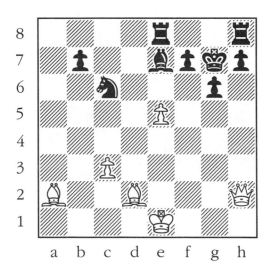

## 179.

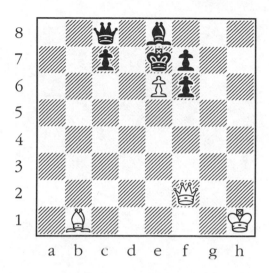

## 180.

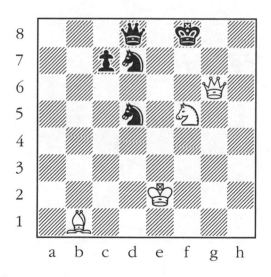

## 181.

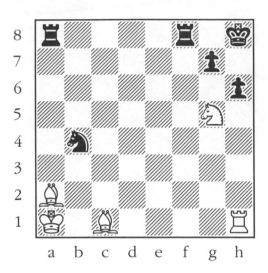

## 182.

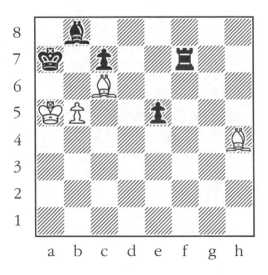

### 183.

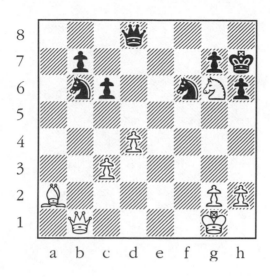

### 184.

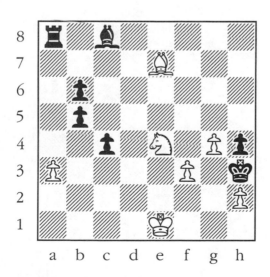

**185.**

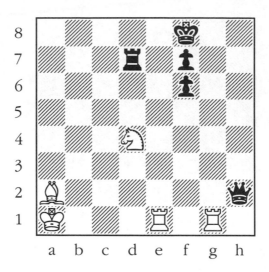

**186.**

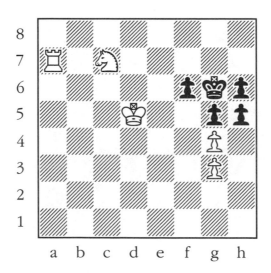

**187.**

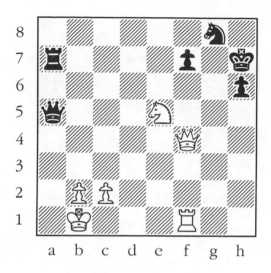

**188.**

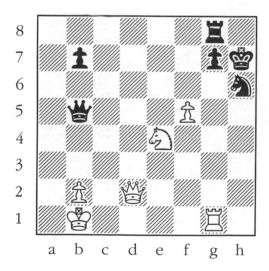

### 189.

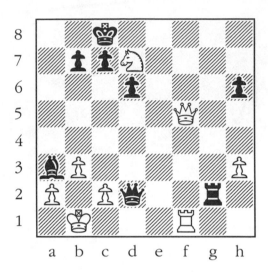

### 190.

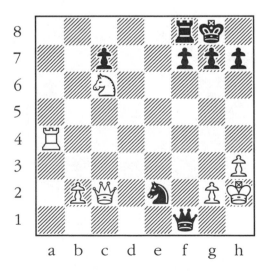

**191.**

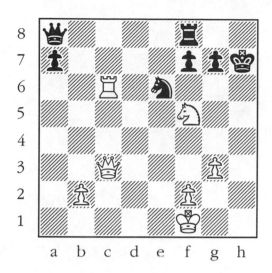

**192.**

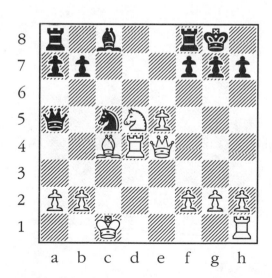

**193.**

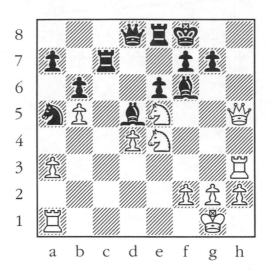

**194.**

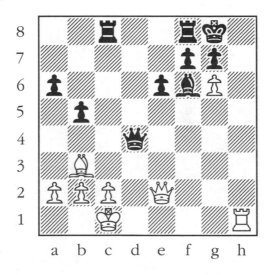

## 195.

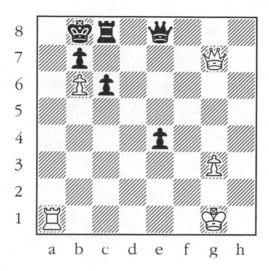

## 196.

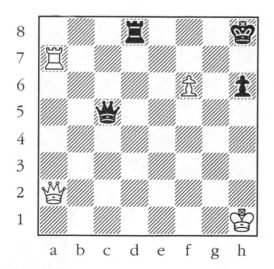

**197.**

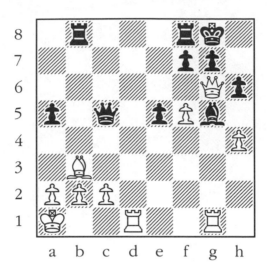

**198.**

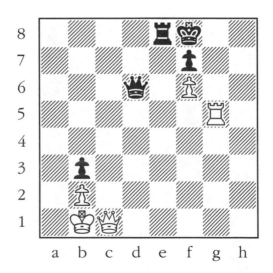

### 199.

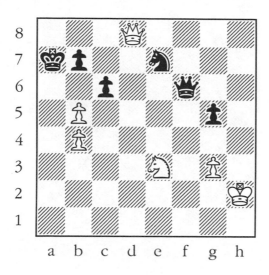

### 200.

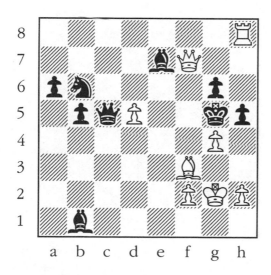

## 201.

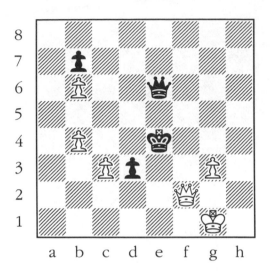

## 202.

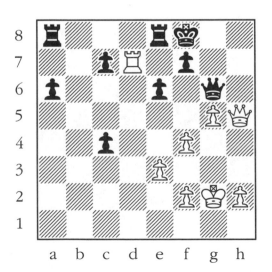

**203.**

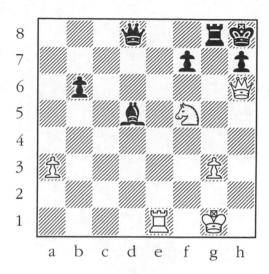

**204.**

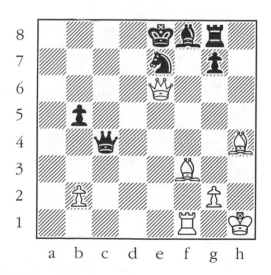

## 205.

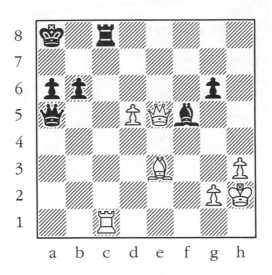

## 206.

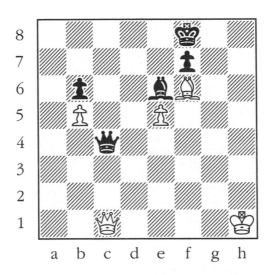

## 207.

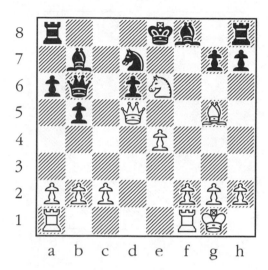

## 208.

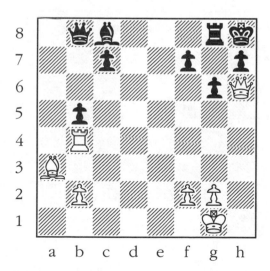

**209.**

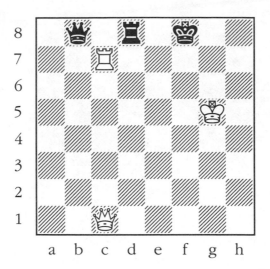

**210.**

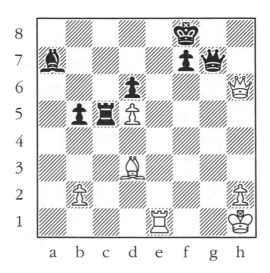

**211.**

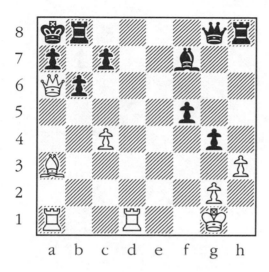

**212.**

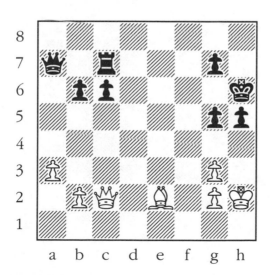

**213.**

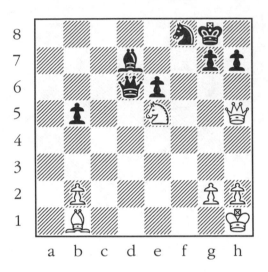

**214.**

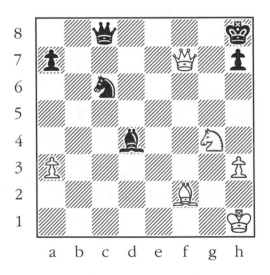

**215.**

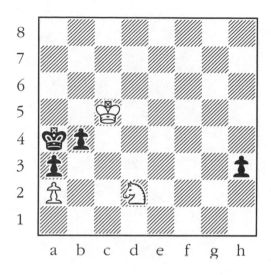

**216.**

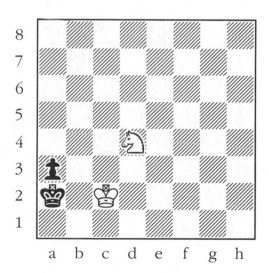

## 217.

## 218.

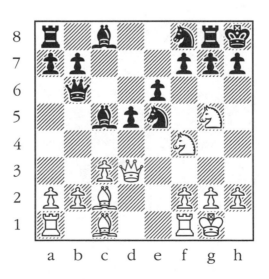

## 219.

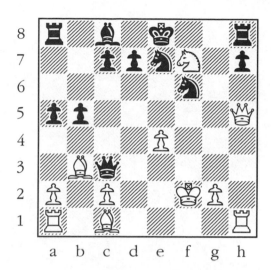

## 220.

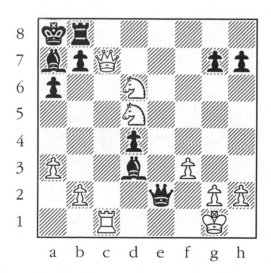

### 221.

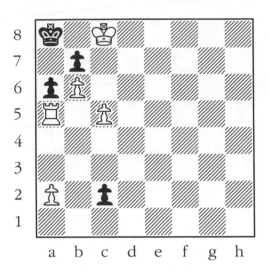

### 222.

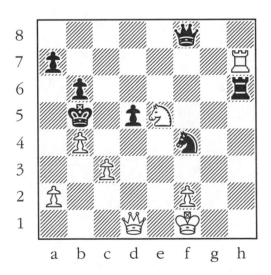

**223.**

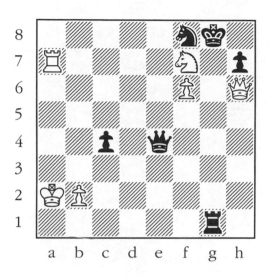

**224.**

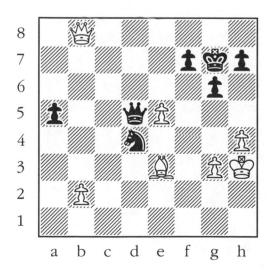

## 225.

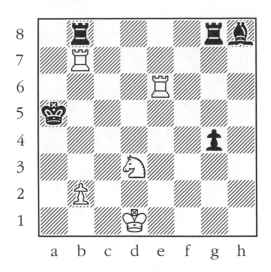

## 226.

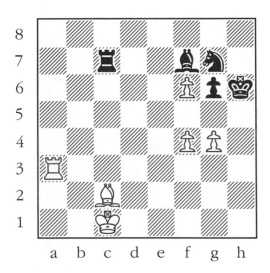

### 227.

### 228.

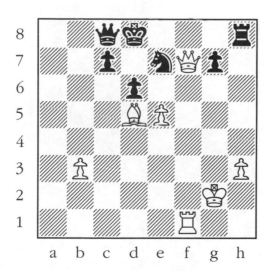

**229.**

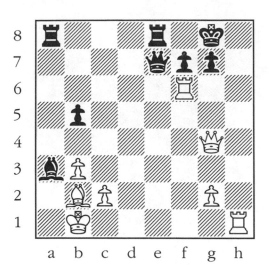

**230.**

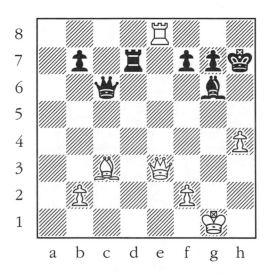

## 231.

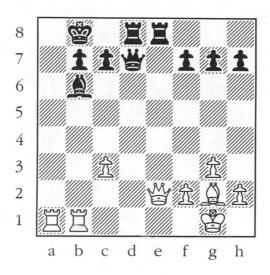

## 232.

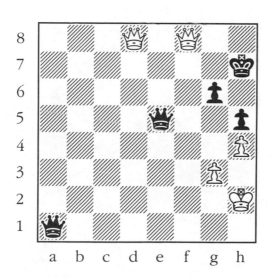

**233.**

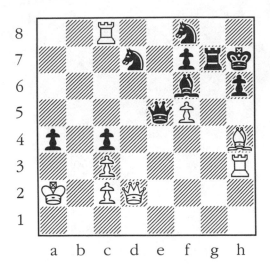

**234.**

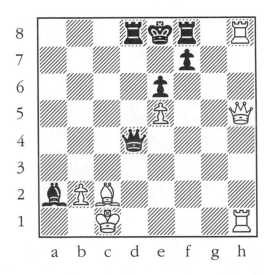

**235.**

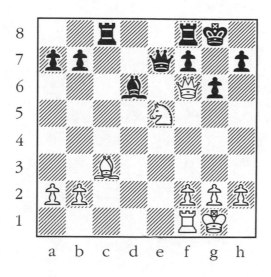

**236.**

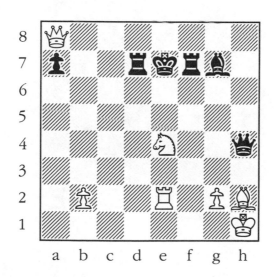

**237.**

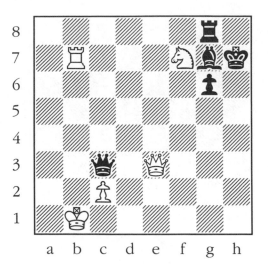

**238.**

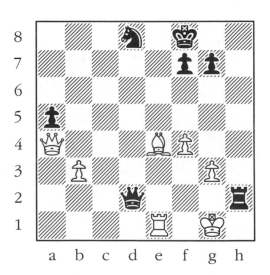

**239.**

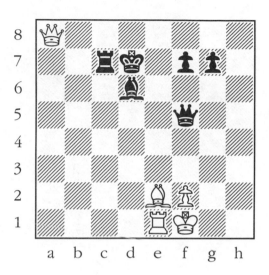

**240.**

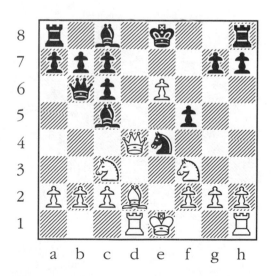

**241.**

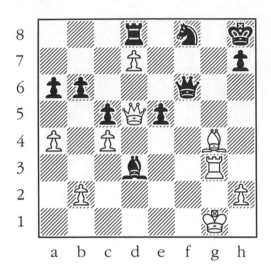

**242.**

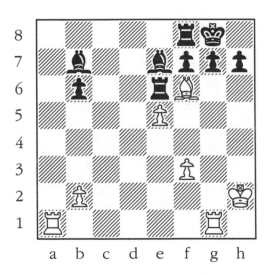

**243.**

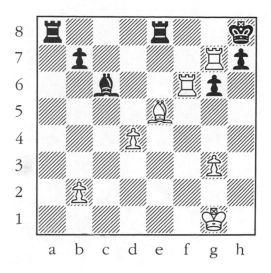

**244.**

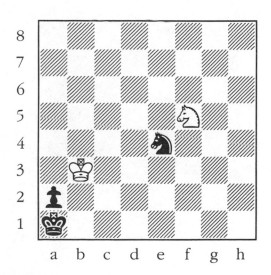

## 245.

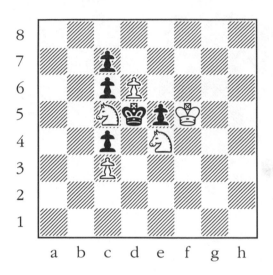

## 246.

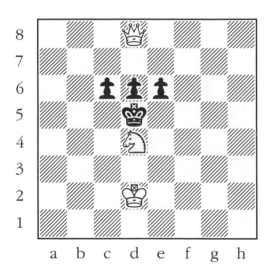

**247.**

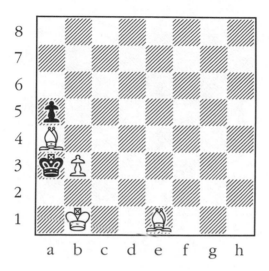

**248.**

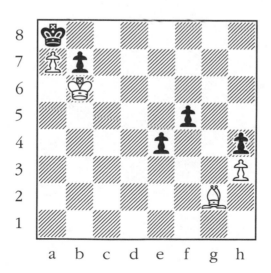

## 249.

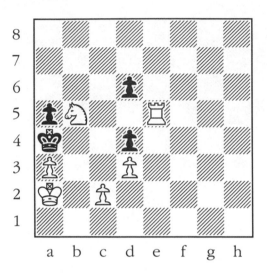

## 250.

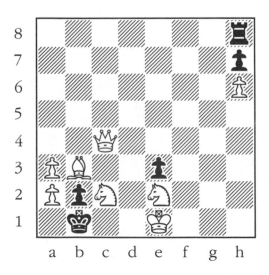

# CHAPTER 4

## BLACK TO MOVE AND MATE IN THREE

### BLACK MATES IN THREE

It's Black's turn again. The sequence is Black, White, Black, White, Black. This third Black move is mate.

The problems in this section are harder than those in the preceding chapter. Black's job always seems to be tougher than White's due to White's inherent advantage in going first. More ingenuity is required, more calculation as well. But you should be up to the task.

### ORGANIZATION

The positions have been randomized for the greatest challenges.

### SOLVING HINTS

The time has come to give away the biggest secret of all: the answers are in the back of the book. So, if you get stuck on a mate, look it up. Then let some time go by, come back, and try again.

## 251.

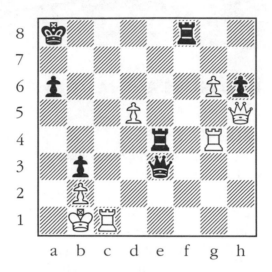

## 252.

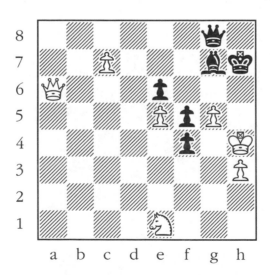

**253.**

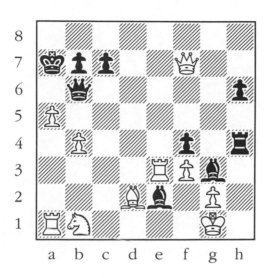

**254.**

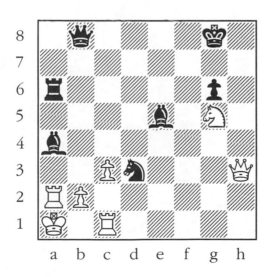

**255.**

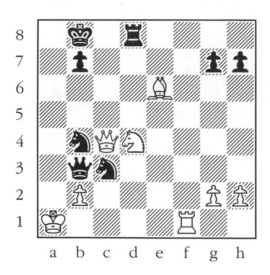

**256.**

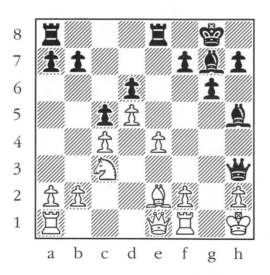

## 257.

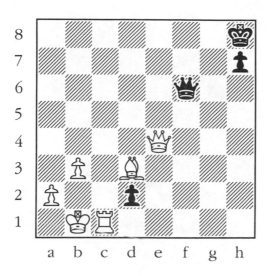

## 258.

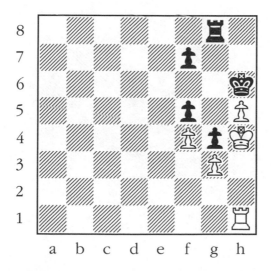

259.

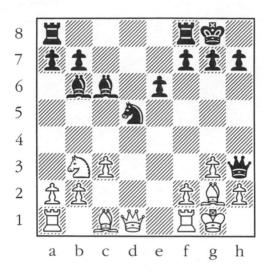

260.

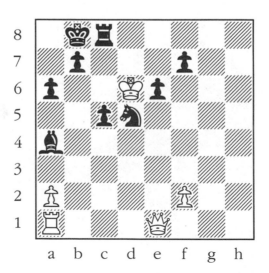

**261.**

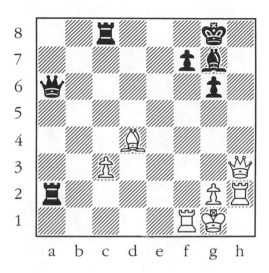

**262.**

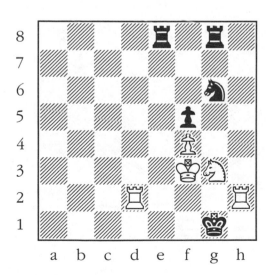

## 263.

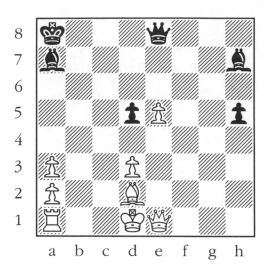

## 264.

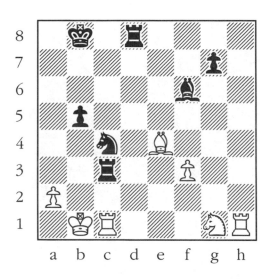

**265.**

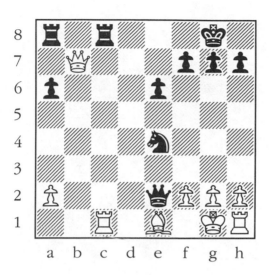

**266.**

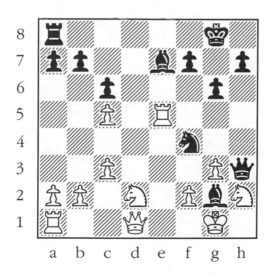

**267.**

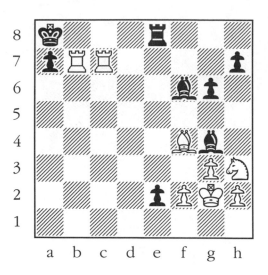

**268.**

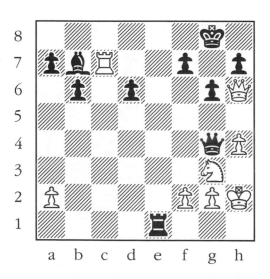

## 269.

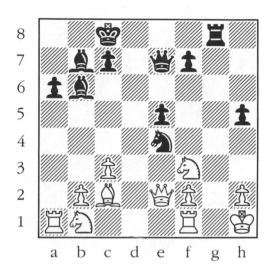

## 270.

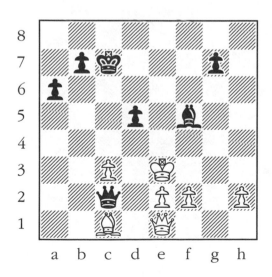

## 271.

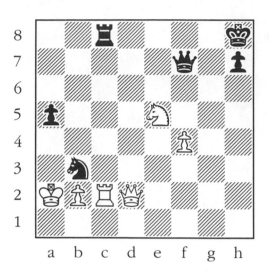

## 272.

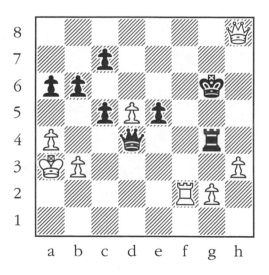

**273.**

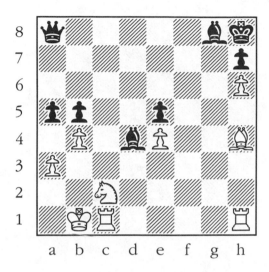

**274.**

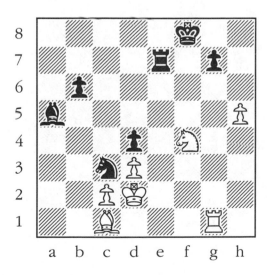

**275.**

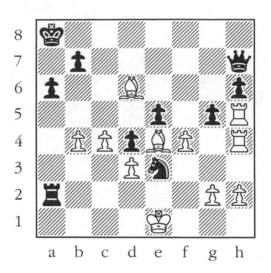

**276.**

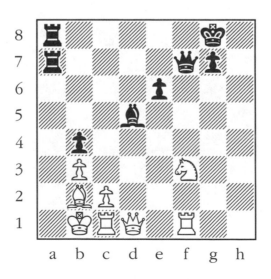

**277.**

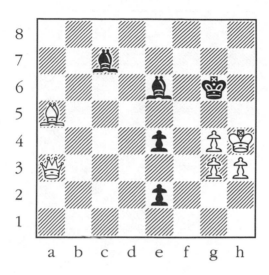

**278.**

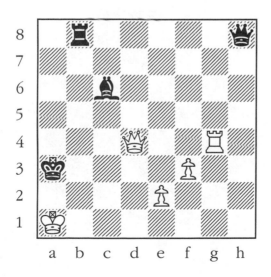

## 279.

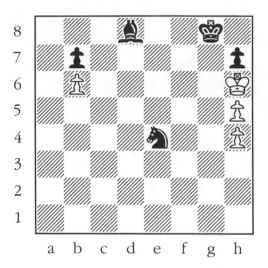

## 280.

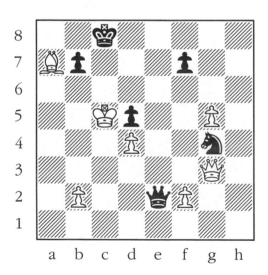

## 281.

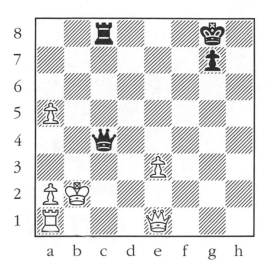

## 282.

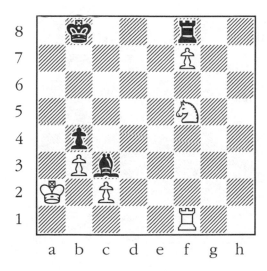

## 283.

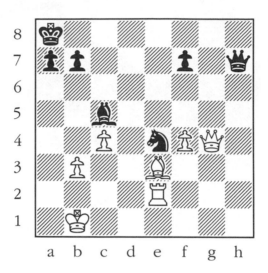

## 284.

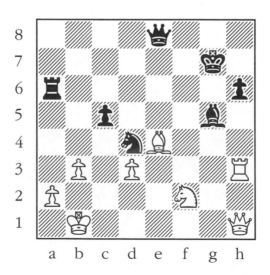

**285.**

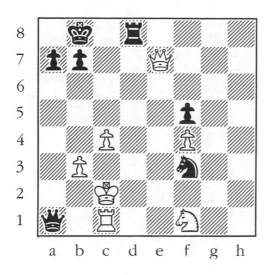

**286.**

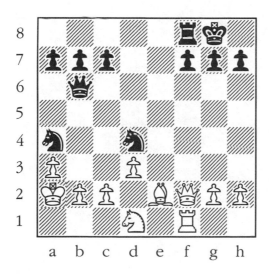

### 287.

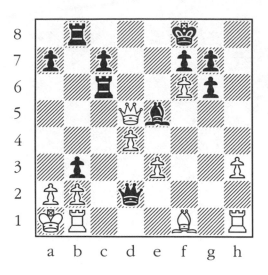

### 288.

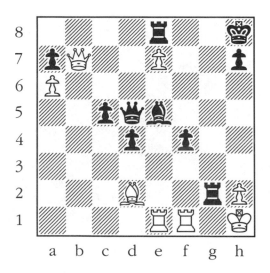

**289.**

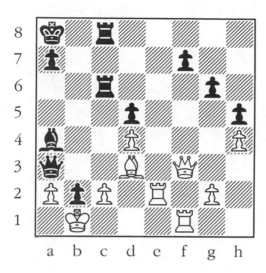

**290.**

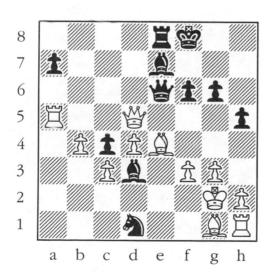

## 291.

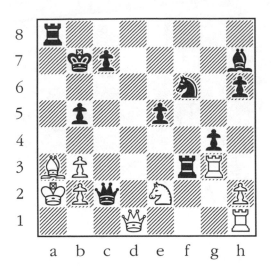

## 292.

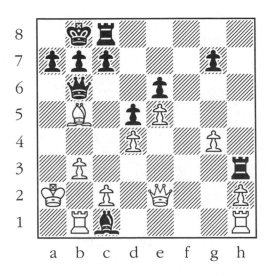

### 293.

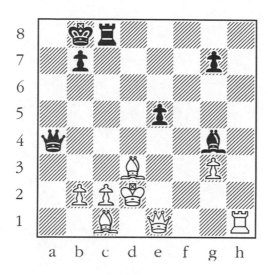

### 294.

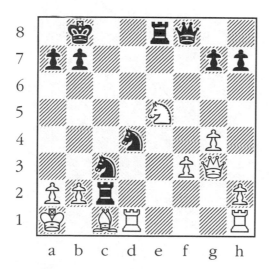

## 295.

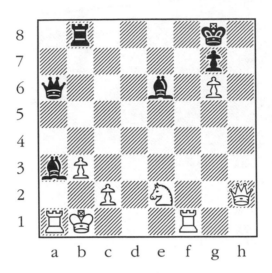

## 296.

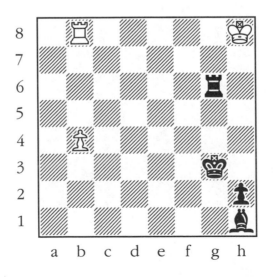

## 297.

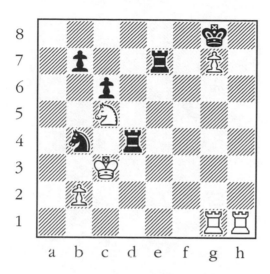

## 298.

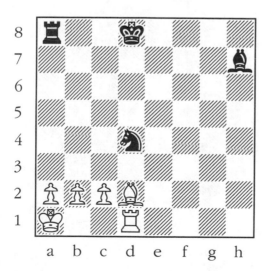

**299.**

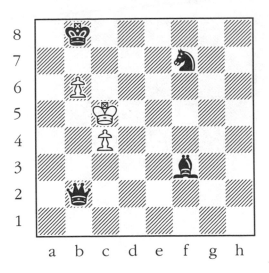

**300.**

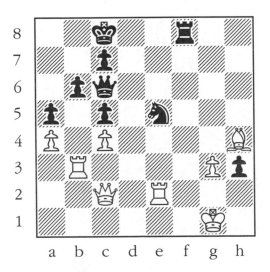

# CHAPTER 5

## WHITE TO MOVE AND MATE IN FOUR

### WHITE MATES IN FOUR

You are about to enter the exalted realm of the four mover. White goes first, Black responds, you know the rest. Mate comes with White's fourth move.

Battle-hardened by your journey through the tricky mates in this book, you are no doubt expecting a reward for all your noble efforts. The big payoff will come when you apply what you've learned to your own games. It's either that or wait for our next book. Meanwhile, we offer a few tasty morsels for your last challenges.

**301.**

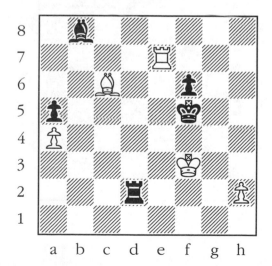

## 302.

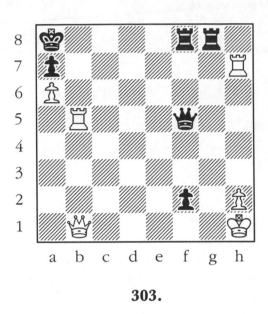

## 303.

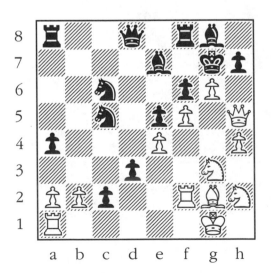

# SOLUTIONS

#1. **1. Ng6+ fxg6 2. Qe8#**

#2. **1. Qf6** *and* **2. Rg8#**

#3. **1. Qxe5+**
   (A) **1...Kg8 2. Qg7#**
   (B) **1...Rxe5 2. Rxd8#**

#4. **1. R1e8** (*threatens* **2. Rxg8#**)
   **1...Rxe8 2. Rxe8#**

#5. **1. Rh8+ Kxh8 2. Rf8#**

#6. **1. Qb8+ Kxb8 2. Rd8#**

#7. **1. Nf6** (*threatens* **2. Qh7#**)
   **1...Bxf6 2. Qxh6#**

#8. **1. Rxf6+**
   (A) **1...gxf6 2. Qxf6#**
   (B) **1...Ke7 2. Rf7#**
   *Double check and mate.*

#9. **1. Qxh5+ Kxh5 2. Rh7#**

#10. **1. Qxh6+ (A) 1...Kg8 2. Rg5#**
   (B) **1...Kxh6 2. Rh5#**

#11. **1. Rh1+ Kg3 2. Rh3#**

#12. **1. Ne5+ Kxd4 2. Rd2#**

#13. **1. Rhh7** *and* **2. Rhe7#**

#14. **1. Qxe8 Kxe8 2. Rd8#**

#15. **1. Bg6+ Kg8 2. Re8#**

#16. **1. Bh6** *and* **2. Rxf8#**

#17. **1. Rf1** *and* **2. Rf8#**

#18. **1. Qxe6+**
   (A) **1...Kh8 2. Qxe8#**
   (B) **1...Rxe6 2. Rf8#**

#19. **1. Rxh6+**
   (A) **1...Kxh6 2. Qh4#**
   (B) **1...Kg8 2. Rh8#**

#20. **1. Qxh6+**
   (A) **1...Kg8 2. Qh8#**
   (B) **1...Kxh6 2. Rh2#**

#21. **1. Qxh7+ Kxh7 2. Bf8#**

#22. **1. Bh6+ Kh7 2. Bf8#**

#23. **1. Qxh5+ gxh5 2. Rh6#**

#24. **1. Qxh7+ Rxh7 2.Rxh7#**

#25. **1. Rh8+ Bxh8 2. Rh7#**

**177**

#26. **1. Re1+ Kd6 2. Re6#**

#27. **1. Qxf5+ Kxf5 2. Rf4#**

#28. **1. g3+ Kxg3 2. Qf2#**

#29. **1. Bb2+ Kxe4 2. Qf3#**

#30. **1. Rc8+ Qxc8 2. Qxd6#**

#31. **1. Qxe6+**
(A) **1...Qe7 2. Qxe7#**
(B) **1...fxe6 2. Bg6#**

#32. **1. Qxf6+**
(A) **1...Qf7 2. Qxf7#**
(B) **1...gxf6 2. Bh6#**

#33. **1. Qxf6+ gxf6 2. Bxf6#**

#34. **1. Bxf7+ Ke7 2. Bg5#**

#35. **1. Rf8+ Bxf8 2. Bg6#**

#36. **1. Qxh7+ Nxh7 2. Bxh7#**

#37. **1. Qxg6+ hxg6 2. Bxg6#**

#38. **1. Qxh5+ Rxh5 2. Bg6#**

#39. **1. Kh2** (*threatens* **2. g3#**)
**1...g4 2. Be7#**

#40. **1. Bc2+ Kh6 2. Nf7#**

#41. **1. Ngf7+ Kg7 2. Bh6#**

#42. **1. Qh8+ Rxh8 2. Nf6#**

#43. **1. Rd7+ Bxd7 2. Nf7#**

#44. **1. Rxb7+ Nxb7 2. Na6#**

#45. **1. Qe8+ Qxe8 2. Nxf6#**

#46. **1. Nxd6+ Nxd6 2. Ne7#**

#47. **1. Qf8+ Rxf8 2. Ne7#**

#48. **1. Qxh6** (*threatens* **2. Qxg7#**).
**1...gxh6 2. Nxh6#**

#49. **1. Qh6+ gxh6 2. Rh7#**

#50. **1. Qxh7+ Kxh7 2. Rh4#**

#51. **1. Nf5+ Kf8 2. Ra8#**
*Anastasia's Mate*

#52. **1. Qf8+**
(A) **1...Rxf8 2. Ne7#**
(B) **1...Kxf8 2. Rh8#**

#53. **1. Qf7+ Bxf7 2. Nd7#**

#54. **1. Qe7+ Rxe7 2. Nf6#**

#55. **1. Qxh7+ Nxh7 2. Ng6#**

#56. **1. Qe2+ Kg5 2. Qg4#**

#57. **1. Rxa6+ bxa6 2. Qa7#**

#58. **1. a4+ Kxa4 2. Qb3#**

#59. **1. Rf8+ Qxf8 2. Qxh7#**

#60. **1. Qh8+ Kf7 2. Qxg7#**

#61. **1. Bxh7+ Qxh7 2. Qf8#**

**178**

#62. **1. Rxa7+ Kxa7 2. Qxb6#**

#63. **1. Bf6** *and* **2. Qe7#**

#64. **1. Rxg7+ Kxg7 2. Qh7#**

#65. **1. Nxe5 Rxe5 2. Nf4#**

#66. **1. Qg8+ Rxg8 2. Nf7#**
*The old Smothered Mate*

#67. **1. Qxh7+ Bxh7 2. Nf7#**

#68. **1. Qxb8+ Qxb8 2. Nb6#**

#69. **1. Qxc7+ Rxc7 2. Nb6#**

#70. **1. Rf5+ (A) 1...Rg5 2. Rxg5#**
**(B) 1...N(B)xf5 2. Nf4#**

#71. **1. Qg7+ Rxg7 2. Nh6#**

#72. **1. Qe4+ Kxe4 2. Nf6#**

#73. **1. Rg8+ Rxg8 2. Nf7#**

#74. **1. e8/N+ Ke6 2. d5#**

#75. **1. fxg7+ Kg8 2. gxh8/Q#**
*Also a pin mate, as the f7 - Knight cannot capture.*

#76. **1. Qg7+ Kxg7 2. h8/Q#**

#77. **1. Rh7+ Kg5 2. h4#**

#78. **1. Qxh5+ Bxh5 2. g5#**

#79. **1. Ra4 Qxa4 2. Qh3#**

#80. **1. Bc5** *(threatens 2. B(Q)xe7#)*
**1...Qxc5 2. Qe8#**

#81. **1. Qxf7+ Kh7 2. Qh5#**

#82. **1. Qxh6+ Kg8 2. Q(R)xg7#**

#83. **1. Qxf7+**
**(A) 1...Kh8 2. Qxf8#**
**(B) 1...Rxf7 2. Rc8#**

#84. **1. Rxh7+ (A) 1...Bxh7 2. Nf7#**
**(B) 1....Kxh7 2. Rh3#**

#85. **1. Qg6** *(threatens 2. Qxh6#)*
**1...Rf8 2. Qxg7#**

#86. **1. Rh6+ e6 2. Nf5#**

#87. **1. Qg6+ Qxg6 2. Rh4#**

#88. **1. Be7+ Kh8 2. Bf6#**

#89. **1. Rf8+ Kxf8 2. Qf7#**

#90. **1. Qh7+ Kxh7 2. Bf7#**

#91. **1. Qg7+ Kxg7 2. Rxg6#**

#92. **1. Qxd8+ Kxd8 2. Rg8#**

#93. **1. c4 Ka5 2. Qa7#**
*The en passent capture, 1...bxc3, is illegal, as the b4 pawn is pinned.*

#94. **1. f4** *and* **2. Nd2#**

#95. **1. Kh6** *and* **2. Rd8#**
*Not 1. Kf6? cxb5! and the d6-Rook is pinned.*

#96.  **1. Kc4** (*threatens* **2. Ra1#**)
    **1...Bxe5  2. Ra6#**

#97.  **1. Kc2** *and* **2. Re1#**

#98.  **1. Nf5** (*threatens* **2. Qg7#**)
    **1...gxf5  2.Qf6#**

#99.  **1. Ba7  c6  2. Bb8#**
    *The Switchback theme.*

#100.  **1. Rh7** *and* **2. R(x)d7#**
    *Black is in zugswang and his rook
    has to give up control of d7.*

#101.  **1...Bh3+  (A) 2. Kxh3  Qg4#**
     **(B)  2. Kg1  Qd4#**

#102.  **1...Qh6+  (A) 2. Kxh6  Bd2#**
     **(B)  2. Bxh6  Bd8#**
     **(C)  2  Kh4  Be1#**

#103.  **1...Ba3** *and* **2...Rc1#**

#104.  **1...Bxf5** (*threatening* **2...Rh3#**)
     **2. Rxf5  R7g4#**

#105.  **1...Qxe2**
     **(A) 2. Rexe2  Rf1#**
     **(B) 2. Rhxe2  Nf2#**
     **(C) 2. Qxe2  Nb2#**

#106.  **1...Bd5+** *and* **2...Qe3#**

#107.  **1...Nc3  (A) 2. Bxb8  Rxa2#**
     **(B) 2. Qxa7  Rb1#**

#108.  **1...Qg1+  2. Nxg1  Nf2#**

#109.  **1...Kh7** *and* **2...g6#**

#110.  **1...Qg1+**
     **(A) 2. Kf3  Bb7#**
     **(B) 2. Kd2  Ne4#**

#111.  **1...Bxb3+**
     **(A) 2. Kxb3  Qa4#**
     **(B) 2. Kb1  Qa2#**
     **(C) 2. Kd2  Qh6#**

#112.  **1...Bc3+**
     **(A) 2. Kxc3  d1/N#**
     **(B) 2. Kb1  d1/Q#**

#113.  **1...Ng3+  2. hxg3  Rh5#**

#114.  **1...Rb2** *and* **2...Rc6#**

#115.  **1...Bf4+  (A) 2. Qxf4  Qa5#**
     **(B) 2. Re3  Rd1#**

#116.  **1...Qa6  (A) 2. g6  Qxg6#**
     **(B) 2. e6  Qxe6#**
     **(C) 2. Ke4  Qd3#**

#117.  **1...Qf1+  (A) 2. Kxf1  Rh1#**
     **(B) 2. Rxf1  Ne2#**

#118.  **1...Nb3+  (A) 2. Bxb3  Qa1#**
     **(B) 2. Kb1  Ned2#**

#119.  **1...b3  (A) 2. cxb3  Kxb3#**
     **(B) 2. Ba2  Kxc2#**

#120.  **1...Qa4+  2. Kd3  Nc1#**

#121.  **1...b5+** *and* **2...Qa6#**

#122.  **1...Rxe2** *and* **2...Be8#**

#123.  **1...Rf5+  (A) 2. Kxe4  Re5#**
     **(B) 2. Kc4  Nd2#**

#124. **1...Qa7** *and* **2...Rxf1#**

#125. **1...gxh1/B 2. Kxg1 Ke2#**

#126. **1...Bb2** (A) **2. Bxb4 Qa1#**
(B) **2. Bxb2 Qa2#**

#127. **1...Qg1+ 2. Kxg1 Re1#**

#128. **1...Rxa3+** (A) **2. Kxa3 Qa1#**
(B) **2. Qxa3 Qa5#**
(C) **2. Kb5 a6#**

#129. **1...Kh1** *zugswang*.
(A) **2. Ne2-***moves* **Ng3#**
(B) **2. Nc4-***moves* **Ne3#**

#130. **1...Qc4+**
*There are eight ways to take the Queen:*
(A) **2. Kxc4 Re4#**
(B) **2. Qxc4 Ne2#**
(C) **2. R6xc4 Ne6#**
(D) **2. R3xc4 Rxd3#**
(E) **2. Bxc4 Nxc6#**
(F) **2. Naxc4 Nxb5#**
(G) **2. Nbxc4 Rd5#**
(H) **2. dxc4 Re4#**

#131. **1...Nf3** (*threatens* **2...Nh2#**)
**2. gxf3 Qh3#**

#132. *White has just played* **1. b2-b4**
*allowing the en passant capture:*
**1...cxb3+ 2. Ka1 Bb2#**

#133. **1...Rxh3+** (A) **2. Kxh3 Qh5#**
(B) **2. gxh3 Qf2#** *An epaulet
mate.*

#134. **1...Nb3** *and* **2...Qa1#**

#135. **1...Ng2** (*threatens* **2...Ne3#**)
**2. Kxg2 f1/Q#**

#136. **1...Nd4+** (A) **2. Kf1 Qg2#**
(B) **2. Bxd4** (*or* **2. Kd2**)
**2...Qd3#**

#137. **1...Qxc5+ 2. Kxc5 Ne6#**

#138. **1...Rxe4** (*threatens* **2...Re1#** *and*
**2...Ref4#**)
(A) **2. Rxe4 Bxe4#**
(B) **2. Rh8+ Re8#**

#139. **1. Be3** *zugswang*.
(A) **2. Nb2 Bc5#**
(B) **2. Nb4 Bc1#**

#140. **1...Nd5** (*threatening* **2...Rd1#**)
*The Knight has to be taken and
there are eight ways to do it:*
(A) **2. Kxd5 Rd1#**
(B) **2. Qxd5 Qa1#**
(C) **2. Rxd5 Qxc4#**
(D) **2. Bxd5 e5#**
(E) **2. Ncxd5 Nxe6#**
(F) **2. Nfxd5 Rxe4#**
(G) **2. exd5 Be5#**
(H) **2. cxd5 Qd3#**

#141. **1.Qc4** (*threatens* **2...Qe2#**)
(A) **2. Bd3 Qxc1#**
(B) **2. Bd1 Qh4#**

#142. **1...Rxf1+ 2. Kxf1 Qh1#**

#143. **1...Rb4** *and* **2...Raxa4#**

#144. **1...Rf5+**
(A) **2. Kxf5 Qf6#**
(B) **2. Ke3 Qe1#**
*A swallow's tail and an epaulet.*

#145. **1...Qh3+**
(A) **2. Kxh3 Bf1#**
(B) **2. Kg1 Qf1#**

#146. **1...Re2+ 2. Kxe2 Qd2#**
*The Swallow's Tail mate, a close relative of the epaulet.*

#147. **1...Qg2+ (A) 2. Qxg2 Ne2#**
**(B) 2. Rxg2 Nh3#**

#148. **1...Qe5** (*threatening* 2...Rd1#.)
**(A) 2. Qxh4+ Rxh4#**
**(B) 2. Qh2 Rf4#**
**(C) 2. Qe1 Rd2#**
**(D) 2. Kb2 Rc4#**
**(E) 2. exd4 Qxd4#**

#149. **1...Rd1+ (A) 2. Nxd1 Qc4#**
**(B) 2. Qe1 Rxe1#**
**(C) 2. Ke2 Nd4#**

#150. **1...b5** (*threatens* 2...Rf1#)
**(A) 2. Qxb5 Qxb5#**
**(B) 2. c3 Qe4#**

#151. **1.Nf4+ Kg8 2. Rag2+ Kf8**
**3. Rh8#**

#152. **1. Qg7+ Rxg7 2. Re8+ Rg8**
**3. Rxg8#**

#153. **1. Nh6+ gxh6 2. Rg3+ Kf7**
(*or* 2...Kh8 3. Rxf8#) **3. Re7#**

#154. **1. Qxf6+ Rxf6**
(*or* 1...Kg8 2. Qg7#) **2. Rxd8+ Rf8 3. Rxf8#**

#155. **1. Qxf7+ Rxf7 2. Rd8+ Rf8 3.Rxf8#**

#156. **1. Qd8 Rxd8 2. f8/Q+ Rxf8 3. Rxf8#**

#157. **1. Nh6+ gxh6 2. Rg4+ Kh8 3. Rxf8#**

#158. **1. Qxb8 Rxb8 2. e8/Q+ Rxe8 3. Rxe8#**

#159. **1. Qxd8+ Rxd8 2. Re8+ Rxe8 3.Rxe8#**

#160. **1. g6+ hxg6 2. fxg6+ Ke8 3. Re8#**

#161. **1. Nh5+ gxh5 2. Qg5+ Kf8 3. Rd8#**

#162. **1. Qh7+ Ka1 2. Qh8 Kb1 3. Qh1#**

#163. **1. Nd7+ Ka8 2. Rc5** (*threatens* 3. Ra5#) **2...Re5 3. Rc8#**

#164. **1. Qxh7+ Kxh7 2. Rh4+ Bxh4 3.Rxh4#**

#165. **1. Ng6+ hxg6 2. Qg1** *and* **3. Qh2#**

#166. **1. Rxh6+ Kxh6 2. Qf4+** *and* **3. Qh2#**

#167. **1. Bg8** (*threatens* 2. Rh7#) **1...Rxg8 2. Rxg8+ Kh7 3. R1g7#**

#168. **1. Rg7+ Kh8 2. Rh7+ Kg8 3. Rag7#**

#169. **1. Qxh7+ Kxh7 2. Rh3+ Kg6 3. Rg2#**

#170. **1. Qh8+ Ke7 2. Ng6+ fxg6 3. Qxg7#**

#171. **1. Qg4+ Bg5 2. Qxg5+ fxg5 3. Rh8#**

**#172.** **1. Qh8+ Kxh8 2. Rxh5+ Kg8 3. Rh8#**

**#173.** **1. Qxb6+ cxb6 2. Rxb6+ Kc7 3. Rb7#**
*The swallow's tail mate.*

**#174.** **1. Qxf8+ Kxf8 2. Bh6+ Kg8 3. Re8#**

**#175.** **1. Qg7+ Bxg7 2. Rxd8+ Bf8 3. Rxf8#**

**#176.** **1. Rf4+ Kh8 2. Ng6+ hxg6 3.Rh4#**
*Greco's h-file corridor mate with Bishop and heavy piece. It goes back to 1619.*

**#177.** **1. Bf5** *followed by* **2. h4+** *and* **3. Rh7#**

**#178.** **1. Bh6+ Kg8 2. Bxf7+ Kxf7 3. Qa2#**

**#179.** **1. Qc5+ Kd8 2. e7+ Kd7 3. Bf5#**

**#180.** **1. Qg7+ Ke8 2. Nd6+ cxd6 3. Bg6#**

**#181.** **1. Rxh6+ gxh6 2. Bb2+ Rf6 3. Bxf6#**

**#182.** **1. Bd8** *followed by* **2. b6+ cxb6 3. Bxb6#** *Black can't stop it.*

**#183.** **1. Nf8+ Kh8 2. Qh7+ Nxh7 3. Ng6#**

**#184.** *The quiet move,* **1. Kf1,** *sets things up:*

**1...Kxh2 2. Bd6+ Kh1 3.Nf2#**
*If Black plays a different first move, White reverses with* **2. Nf2+** *and* **3. Bd6#**

**#185.** **1. Re8+ Kxe8 2. Rg8+ Ke7 3. Nf5#**

**#186.** **1. Ne8** *(threatens* **2. Rg7#)**
**1...hxg4 2. Rg7+**
**(A) 2. ...Kf5 3. Nd6#**
**(B) 2. ...Kh5 3. Nxf6#**

**#187.** **1. Qxf7+ Rxf7 2. Rxf7+ Kh8 3. Ng6#**

**#188.** **1. Qxh6+ gxh6**
**(1...Kxh6 2. Rh1#) 2. Nf6+ Kh8 3. Rxg8#**
*The Arabian Rook and Knight mate.*

**#189.** **1. Nc5+ Kb8 (1...Kd8 2. Qd7#) 2. Qc8+ (A) 2...Ka7 2. Qxb7#) (B) 2...Kxc8 3.Rf8#**

**#190.** **1. Ne7+ Kh8 2. Qxh7+ Kxh7 3. Rh4#** *Anastasia's mate.*

**#191.** **1. Qxg7+ Nxg7 2. Rh6+ Kg8 3. Ne7#**

**#192.** **1. Ne7+ Kh8 2. Qxh7+ Kxh7 3. Rh4#**

**#193.** **1. Qxf7+ Rxf7 2. Ng6+ Kg8 3. Rh8#**

**#194.** **1. Rh8+ Kxh8 2. Qh5+ Kg8 3. Qh7#**

#195. **1. Ra8+ Kxa8 2. Qa1+ Kb8
3. Qa7#**

#196. **1. Rh7+ Kxh7 2. Qf7+ Kh8
3. Qg7#**

#197. **1. Rxg5** (*threatens* **2. Qxg7#**)
**1. ...hxg5 2. f6** *and* **3. Qxg7#**

#198. **1. Rg8+ Kxg8 2. Qg5+ Kf8
3. Qg7#**

#199. **1. b6+ Ka6 2. Qa8+ Kb5
3. Qa5#**

#200. **1. h4+ Kxh4 2. Rxh5+ gxh5
3. Qxh5#**

#201. **1. Qf4+ Kd5 2. c4+ Kc6
3. Qc7#**

#202. **1. Qh8+ Qg8 2. Rxf7+ Kxf7
3. Qf6#** *The swallow's tail mate.*

#203. **1. Re8** (*threatens* **2. Qg7#**)
**1...Qxe8 2. Qf6+ Rg7
3. Qxg7#**

#204. **1. Bc6+ Qxc6 (1...Kd8 2. Qd7#)
2. Rxf8+ Kxf8 3. Qxe7#**

#205. **1. Rxc8+ Bxc8 2. Bf4** *and*
**3. Qb8#**

#206. **1. Qh6+ Ke8 (1...Kg8 2. Qg7#)
2. Qh8+ Kd7 3. Qd8#**

#207. **1. Nc7+ Qxc7 2. Qe6+ Be7
3. Qxe7#**

#208. **1. Rh4 Rg7 2. Bf8** *and the
Queen mates on g7 or h7.*

#209. **1. Qf4+ Kg8 2. Qf7+ Kh8
3. Qg7#**

#210. **1. Qxd6+ Kg8 2. Re8+ Qf8
3. Qxf8#**

#211. **1. Bf8** (*threatens* **2. Qxa7#**)
**1...Rb7
2. Rd8+ Rb8 3. Qxa7#**

#212. **1. Bxh5** (*threatens* **2. Qg6#**)
**1...Kxh5 2. Qh7+ Kg4 3. Qh3#**

#213. **1. Bxh7+ Nxh7 (1...Kh8 2.Nf7#)
2. Qf7+ Kh8 3. Ng6#**

#214. **1. Bxd4+ Nxd4 2. Qf6+ Kg8
3. Nh6#**

#215. **1. Nb3 h2 2. Kb6 h1/Q
3. Nc5#**

#216. **1. Ne2 Ka1 2. Nc1 a2
3. Nb3#**

#217. **1. Rh3 gxh3 (1...g3 2. Ng4#)
2. Ng4 h2 3 Nf2#**

#218. **1. Qxh7+ Nxh7 2. Nxf7+ Nxf7
3. Ng6#**
*White's 1st and 2nd moves can be
reversed.*

#219. **1. Nd6+ Kd8 (1...Kf8 2. Qh6#)
2. Qe8+ Rxe8 3. Nf7#**

#220. **1.Qxb8+Bxb8 (1...Kxb8 2.Rc8#)
2. Nb6+ Ka7 3. Ndc8#**

#221. **1. Rxa6+ bxa6 2. b7+ Ka7
3. b8/Q#**

#222. **1. Qa4+ Kxa4 2. Rxa7+ Kb5
3 a4#**

#223. **1. Qg7+ Rxg7 2. Nh6+ Kh8
3. fxg7#**

#224. **1. Bh6+ Kxh6 2. Qf8+ Kh5
3. g4#**

#225. **1. Ra6+ Kxa6 2. Nc5+ Ka5
3. b4#**

#226. **1. Rh3+ Nh5 2. Rxh5+ gxh5
3. g5#**

#227. **1. Nh5+ Kg8 2. f6 hxg5 3. f7#**

#228. **1. Qf8+ Rxf8 2. Rxf8+ Kd7
3. e6#**

#229. **1. Rh8+ Kxh8 2. Rh6+ Kg8
3. Qxg7#**

#230. **1. Rh8+ Kxh8 2. Qh6+ Bh7
3. Qxg7#**

#231. **1. Ra8+ Kxa8 2. Qa6+ Kb8
3. Qxb7#**

#232. **1. Qg8+ Kh6 2. Qdf8+ Qg7
3. Qh8#**

#233. **1. Qxh6+ Kg8 (1...Kxh6
2.Bxf6#) 2. Bxf6 Rh7** (*else
Queen mates at g7 or h8*)
**3. Qxh7#** *A pin mate.*

#234. **1. Qxf7+ Kxf7 2. R1h7+ Ke8
3. Bg6#**

#235. **1. Qh8+ Kxh8 2. Nxf7+ Kg8
3. Nh6#**

#236. **1. Qe8+ Kxe8 2. Nf6+ Kd8
3. Re8#**

#237. **1. Qh6+ Bxh6 2. Ng5+ Kh8
3. Rh7#**

#238. **1. Qe8+ Kxe8 2. Bc6+ Kf8
3. Re8#**

#239. **1. Qe8+ Kxe8 2. Bb5+ Kd8
3. Re8#**

#240. **1. Qd8+ Kxd8 2. Bg5+ Ke8
3. Rd8#**

#241. **1. Qg8+ Kxg8 2. Be6+ Kh8
3. Rg8#**

#242. **1. Rxg7+ Kxg7 2. Rg8+ Kxg8
3. Rg1#**

#243. **1. Rf8+ Rxf8 2. Rxg6+ Rf6
3. Bxf6#**

#244. **1. Kc2 Nd2 2. Nd4 N-moves
3. Nb3#**

#245. **1. Kf6 cxd6 2. Ke7 dxc5
3. Nf6#**

#246. **1. Kd3 (A) 1...Kc5 2. Qa5#
(B) 1...Ke5 2. Qg5#
(C) 1...c5 2. Qg5+ e5 3. Qg8#
(D) 1...e5 2. Qa5+ c5 3. Qa8#**

#247. 1. **Bf2 Kb4 2. Bd4 Ka3 3.Bc5#**
*A little King and Bishop duel.
Bishop wins.*

#248. **1. Bh1 f4 2. Bxe4 f3 3.Bxb7#**
*A Bishop and Pawn duel. No
contest. Bishop wins again.*

#249. **1. Rc5**
(A) 1...dxc5 2. c4 dxc3
3. Nxc3#
(B) 1...d5 2. c3 dxc3 3. Nxc3#

#250. **1. Qg8 Rxg8 2. Bxg8 Kxc2**
3. Bxh7#

#251. **1...Rf1** (*threatens* 2...Qxc1#)
2. Rxf1 Qe1+ 3. Rxe1 Rxe1#

#252. **1...Bf6** (*threatens* 2...Qxg5#)
2. Nf3 (*or* 2. exf6 *or* 2. gxf6)
2...Kg6 *and* 3...Qh7#
*Black's first move seals the 6th rank so White cannot play Qxe6 with check.*

#253. **1...Qxe3+ 2. Bxe3 fxe3** *and*
3...Bf2#

#254. **1...Qxb2+ 2. Rxb2 Bc2+**
3. Ra2 Bxc3#

#255. **1...Qd1+ 2. Rxd1 Nc2+**
3. Nxc2 Rxd1#

#256. **1...Bf3+ 2.Bxf3** (*or* 2.Kg1 Qg2#)
2...Be5 *and* 3...Qxh2#

#257. **1...Qa1+ 2. Kxa1** (2.Kc2 Qxc1#)
2...dxc1/Q+ 3. Bb1 Qc3#

#258. **1...f6 2. Ra1 Rg5** (*threatens*
3...Rxh5#) 3. fxg5+ fxg5#

#259. **1...Qxg2+ 2. Kxg2 Nf4+**
3. Kg1 Nh3#

#260. **1...Rc6+** (A) 2. Kd7 Rb6+
3. Kd8 Rd6#
(B) 2. Ke5 Bc2 *and* 3...f6#

#261. **1...Bxd4+**
(A) 2. Qe3 Bxe3+ 3. Rf2
(*or* 3. Kh1 Qxf1#) 3...Ra1#
(B) 2. cxd4 Qxf1+ 3. Kxf1 c1#

#262. **1...Nh4+ 2. Rxh4 Rxg3+**
3. Kxg3 Re3#

#263. **1...Qa4+** (A) 2. Kc1 Bxd3
3. Qd1 Qxa3# (B) 2. Ke2
Bxd3+ 3. Kxd3 (*or* 3. Kf3
Qg4#) 3...Qc4#

#264. **1...Rc2** (*threatens* 2...Na3#)
(A) 2. Rxc2 Rd1+ 3. Rc1 Na3#
(B) 2. Kxc2 Rd2+ 3. Kb3 Rb2#

#265. **1...Qxf2+ 2. Bxf2 Rxc1+**
3. Be1 Rxe1#

#266. **1...Be4** (*threatens* 2...Qg2#)
(A) 2. Qf3 Bxf3 *and* 3...Qg2#
(B) 2. Qf1 Ne2+ 3. Qxe2 Qg2#
*From a scholastics tournament. The kid playing Black sat for over twenty minutes and worked it out.*

#267. **1...Bxf3+ 2. Kxf3**
(2. Kg1 e1/Q#)
2...e1/N+ 3. Kg4 h5#

#268. **1...Rh1+ 2. Kxh1 Qh3+**
3. Kg1 Qxg2#

#269. **1...Qg5** (*threatens* 2...Qg2#)
(A) 2. Nxg5 Nxf2+ 3. Kg1
Nh3#
(B) 2. Rg1 Qxg1+ 3. Nxg1
Ng3#

#270. **1...d4+**
(A) 2. Kxd4 Qe4+ 3. Kc5 b6#
(B) 2. cxd4 Qe4+ 3. Kd2 Qxd4#
(C) 2. Kf4 Qe4+ *and* 3...Qg4#

**186**

#271. 1...Nc1+ 2. Kb1 (2. Ka3 Qb3#)
2...Qa2+ 3. Kxc1 Qa1#

#272. 1...Qa1+ 2. Ra2 Rxa4+
3. bxa4 (or 3. Kxa4  Qxa2#)
3...Qc3# *An epaulet mate.*

#273. 1...Ba2+ 2. Kxa2 Qg8+
3. Kb1 Qb3#

#274. 1...Re2+ 2. Nxe2 Ne4+
3. Kd1 Nf2#

#275. 1...Qxe4 (*threatens* 2...Nxg2+
*and* 3...Qe1#)
2. dxe4 d3 *and*
3...Re2# *is unstoppable.*

#276. 1...Ra1+ 2. Bxa1 Qa7 *and*
3...Qa2#

#277. 1...Bd8+ 2. Bxd8 (2. g5 Bxg5#
2...e1/N *with* 3...Ng2# *or else*
3...Nf3#

#278. 1...Be4 (*threatens both* 2...Qxd4#
*and* 2...Rb1#)
2. Rxe4 Qh1+
3. Qd1 Qxd1#

#279. 1...Ng5 (*releases stalemate and
creates zugzswang*)
2. hxg5 Bxb6
3. g6 Be3#

#280. 1...Qc4+ 2. Kd6 (2. Kb6 Qb4#)
2...Qc7+ 3. Kxd5 Qc6#

#281. 1...Qb5+ 2. Ka3 Rc4 (*threatens*
3...Ra4#) 3. Qd1 Qb4#

#282. 1...Kc7 *followed by* 2...Ra8 *and*
3...Ra1# *Not* 1...Rxf7?
*when White  can drag things out
by* 2. Ne7!

#283. 1...Nd2+ (A) 2. Kb2 Qb1+
3. Kc3 Ne4# (B) 2. Kc1 Qb1+
3. Kxd2 Bb4#
*A switch back combined with a
criss-cross mate.*

#284. 1...Qa4 (*threatens* 2...Qxa2#)
(A) 2. a3 Qxb3+ 3. Ka1 Rxa3#
(B) 2. bxa4 Rb6+ 3. Ka1 Nc2#
(C) 2. Kb2 (*or* 2. Re3) 2...
Qxa2+ *and* 3...Qc2#

#285. 1...Rd2+ 2. Nxd2 Qa2+ *and*
3...Qxd2#

#286. 1...Qxb2+ 2. Nxb2 Nc3+
3. Ka1 Nxc2#

#287. 1...Qxb2+ (A) 2. Rxb2 Rc1+
3. Rb1 b2# (B) 2. Kxb2 Rc2+
*and* 3...Rxa2#

#288. 1.Rg1+ 2. Kxg1 Rg8+
3. Kf2 Rg2#

#289. 1...Bb3 (*threatens* 2...Qxa2#)
2. cxb3 (2. axb3 Qa1#) 2...
Rc1+ 3. Rxc1 Rxc1#

#290. 1...Qh3+ 2. Kxh3 Bf1+
3. Kh4 f5#

#291. 1...Rxa3+ 2. Kxa3 Qc5+
3. Ka2 Qa7#
*Greco's mating pattern on the
Rook's file.*

#292. 1...Qa5+ 2. Ba4 Qxa4+
3. bxa4 Ra3#

#293. 1...Rxc2+ 2. Bxc2 Qb4+
3. Ke3 Qd4#

**187**

#294.  1...Nb3+  2. axb3 Qa3+
3. bxa3 Ra2#

#295.  1...Rxb3+  2. cxb3
(2. Ka2 Rb2#)
2...Qd3+  3. Ka2 Qxb3#

#296.  1...Bb7 (*threatens* 2...h1/Q#)
(A) 2. Kh7 Rg4 *and* 3...h1/Q#
(B) 2. Rxb7 h1/Q+  3. Rh7
Qa8#

#297.  1...Re3+  2. Kxd4 Nc2+
3. Kc4 b5#

#298.  1...Nxc2+  2. Kb1 Nd4+
3. Kc1 (*or* 3. Ka1 Nb3#)
3...Ne2#

#299.  1...Ba8  2. b7 Kxb7
3. Kd5 Qe5#

#300.  1...Rf1+  2. Kxf1 Qh1+
3. Kf2 Ng4#

#301.  1. Be4+  Kg5 2. Rg7+  Kh6
3. Rh7+  Kg5  4. h4#

#302.  1. Rxa7+  Kxa7  2. Rb7+  Ka8
3. Ra7+  Kxa7  4. Qb7#

#303.  1. Qh6+  Kxh6  2. Ng4+  Kg7
3. Nh5+  Kh8  4. g7#

# CARDOZA PUBLISHING ONLINE
## www.cardozabooks.com

We welcome your suggestions and comments, and are glad to have you as a customer. Our philosophy is to bring you the best quality chess books from the top authors and authorities in the chess world, featuring *words* (as opposed to hieroglyphics), *clear expanations* (as opposed to gibberish), *nice presentations* (as opposed to books simply slapped together), and authoritative information. And all this at reasonable prices.

We hope you like the results.

Don't forget to try out Cardoza Publishing's fun and instructive chess books by Fred Wilson and Bruce Alberston:
   303 Tricky Tactics
   303 Tricky Checkmates
   303 Tricky Chess Puzzles
   303 Crushing Chess Tactics

To find out about our newest chess and backgammon books:
   Go online: www.cardozabooks.com
   Use email: cardozabooks@aol.com
   Call toll free: (800)577-WINS